A
Poetry Archive

Volume 2
Music, Art, and Magic
1998 - 2003

Frank Prem

Wild Arancini Press
2024

Publication Details

Title: A Poetry Archive -
         Archive Volume 2: Music, Art and Magic - 1998 - 2003

ISBN: 978-1-923166-13-4 (p-bk)
SBN: 978-1-923166-14-1 (e-bk)

Published by Wild Arancini Press
Copyright © 2024 Frank Prem
All rights reserved:

No part of this publication may be reproduced, stored in a retrieval system, or transmitted in any form or by any means, electronic, mechanical, photocopying, recording or otherwise, without prior written permission from the publisher and author.
A catalogue record for this book is available from the National Library of Australia.

Book cover design and formatting by WildAranciniPress.com

Who would not choose music or art? Who would overlook Magic?

CONTENTS

A Poetry Archive Volume 2

Introduction	1
Musical Themes	3
Art	27
The Magic of Writing	51
Places and Locations	95
Portrait Gallery	159
My Neighbourhood	193
After Words	251
Index of Poems	253
Author Information	259
Other Published Works	261
What Readers Say	263

A Poetry Archive Volume 2

Introduction

The A *Poetry Archive* series captures the great majority of formative poetic work undertaken by Frank Prem. Predominantly, this work took place between 1998 and 2003, with instances of both prior and later work included.

The work in these volumes is raw and to some extent follows the development of Prem as an uncertain poet and through to a gradually surer grasp of the craft.

The period from 1998 (and earlier) to 2003 covers a time of intense and extensive development by the poet with regular public reading at 'Spoken Word' venues, such as The Dan O'Connell Hotel in Carlton, as well as competition work and first publications of Prem's poetry in Journals, Newspapers or other Magazines.

The Archive -particularly Volumes 1 and 2 - is constructed to reflect themes where possible (such as Beach and Water, Music, Art and Magic, for example), with some work grouped in simple alphabetical listing.

Dates are given where a record still exists.

Musical Themes

a feeling for song

he has no music
but feeling for song
without a way to share
no notes
no sign of soaring voice
taking flight like a flock
before the rising wind
or a whisper swaying branches no
music he can offer you loud
nothing to sing
nothing to say except that
feeling for song
is enough to sense sound
shouting out
in his head
to make him smile
to make you wonder
at the feeling in your air

June 2001

Frank Prem

a hum for you

i hum deep enough to vibrate
the cavity surrounding my heart
it starts low
near the bottom of my lungs
no words
but a sound to resemble a small tune
running through my head for three days
I'd like to sing for you
to share
but a hum is all the expression
I can give

I find comfort
an underlying smoothness
within the rumbled thrumming of voice
all tone and timbre
can you hear me?

rest your head here
I will create a richness
I will hum
especially for you

September 2001

a song in the dark

darkness is more
than a black hollow space
it is a friend
a dark canvas
to draw in white dreams
to imagine a light
so the lonely
can find a way home

this night in the dark
I'm filling in spaces
with music and song
it is alive
my mind is swaying in time
I raise up my voice
to cry words out loud
but the silence goes on
undisturbed

no-one can see what I've done
nobody can hear
but tonight
in my darkness
I sang

a wailing companion

it is there again
still there

if he was feeling testy
he would describe it as a caterwauling
that will not stop
constant yowling

but today is ok
today it is companionable
a reassurance
that everything is at it should be
and the old wailer
is welcome to perform

nondescript sounds
vaguely musical
mosque in the morning
head space for minaret
something almost religious
in the rise and fall of the sounds

he prefers female music
but the voice
is strong masculine
verbalising in an unknown tongue
no choice in that
though he knows he can block it by work
by hard concentration
but even then
the song might thread the thoughts
while he is only half aware

some days he wants to scream
claw his face and head bloody
to be alone
just for some moments
alone

Musical Themes

today is ok
the singer helps to keep it tolerable
on a good day

October 2002

bamboo and reed

Featured in OZpoet Treasures of the Board March 2001.
Published in The Brown Critique (India) July - October 2001

bamboo and reed
quaver frail wind
tremble declaration
to the sky

blow mellow air
resonate in song
breathe liberation
in a sigh

and play
oh play
play to raise my heart up
on this day of wind and rain
play to bring a hope to me again

bamboo and reed
quaver frail sound
tremble declaration
in a sigh

March 2001

bamboo breeze

it is not a song
just the sound
of wind
blown through a bamboo pipe
into my mind

in the stillest hour
I have ever known
the bamboo breeze
has called

and now is haunting me
to respond

February 2003

brassy slow time (will you dance?)

hey, what's that sound I hear?
I'd like to know.
Somebody playing brass . . . keeping
way down low.
It's dark and on the floor . . . couples
dancing slow,
while I . . .

I am slowly swaying and I . . .
can hear the music saying

Go and get somebody,
anybody who can hold you on the floor
and who can
move you in a slow song,
gentle rhythm of a slow song, if you'll
just let go . . .

Hey, the brass is playing slow time,
would you like to dance?
They're playing it that way so we
can make romance.
It's dark and on the floor . . . lovers
in a trance,
while I . . .

I can see you swaying and you . . .
can hear the music saying

Be a little bolder,
rest your head against my shoulder,
while I hold you and I
move you to a slow song,
gentle rhythm of a slow song, if you'll
take a chance . . .

In brassy slow time,
will you dance?

March 2001

broke-neck guitar

I miss the sound of your guitar
it broke in a pity
at our feet
that day at the airport
what could we do
hold the neck
hug the body
shed a tear
take it home
lay it down to rest on the floor
in the closet with the shoes
and the travel bags

I haven't heard you play
not since Brisbane
except when we borrowed the twelve string
but that doesn't count
the sound wasn't yours
drifting up from the bedroom
where you'd sit in the centre of the bed
with the music spread round your feet

one day I'll surprise you

May 2002

burned in love (yee haw!)

burned in love, who gives a damn?
Burned in love, oh man, oh man!
Burned in love, but what can you do?
Burned in love, it can happen to you.

Burnee #1

I was burned in love
It was a helluva time
Burned in a fire
Eating up my mind.

Thought that love
Was the end of the way
But I burned in love
Just seventeen days.

Burned in love, can you believe it?
Burned in love, but I couldn't leave it
Burned in love, a fool through and through
Burned in love, it might happen to you.

Burnee #2

Love burned me
Melted my heart
I was in love, man
Right from the start.

Love led me
On a merry old dance
But it ended in a bottle
Without romance.

Burned in love, sulfur in the air
Burned in love, I think I singed my hair
Burned in love, I fell on my face
Burned in love at a lightning pace.

Burnee #3

Yes, it burned me
Did it burn you too?
I burned in love
I tell you, it's true.

When the fire went out
I lost my bliss
But, move over honey
I was talkin to Chris...

Burned in love, I'd do it again
Burned in love, right down to the end
Well, I burned in love, watch out, Sue
Mighta burned in love, but I'm lookin at you.

Burnee #4

I burned, too
I have to admit it
Didn't have the sense
To know when to quit it.

Can you hold my head
Just to give it a rest?
Coz, you know, I feel
Another thumpin in my chest.

Burn in love, get in a line
To burn in love, just one more time
Burnin love, I'm ready to go
One more burnin love for the road.

One more love, to burn in the night
Another dose of love to give us a fright
A burnin love - who could ask for more?
Light up that fire, babe, that's what it's for.

Yee Haw!

January 1999

call it music

call it music if you will

Nina Simone   misunderstood
and my boy
sliding into Eagle leathers
soft   hugging skin   tight

earring chain and cross
silver buttons   opened down
to number three
smooth   hairless   shining
ready for the dark red-room at The Laird

my boy and me

call it music   if you will

Nina

I will wear my studded cap

May 2001

Musical Themes

choosing between guitars

i almost wrote a poem about guitars
but I stopped myself in time
because I don't play

what I really wanted to talk a little bit
about was choosing
between new and old
a six string and a twelve that was a gift
to a man with only one pair of hands
and a limit to the time and skills he can apply
to joy extraction and making pleasure

the twelve string is an exotic beast
and it makes a gorgeous sound
if you know what to do
how to stroke it and how to coax
and bend the notes till they break
somebody's heart from an overdose
of listening to melody and sweetness
it can make you sound better

the six string is an old companion
to play with friends that want to sing along
to the same old words of the same old songs
we all know so well
at three A.M. in the morning
because we've practiced for so long
with broken and smoky voices

hard to choose what to keep
and what to send away
when you only have one pair of hands
and a limit to what one man can do
to coax a little joy
extract a small pleasure
and make a hard choice

August 2000

circle dance

he steps around her in a slow circle
he's not watching really
only from the corner of his eye
to never lose her from the sight-line
but he isn't watching her
not really

she's oblivious
hardly attending
what he's doing isn't relevant
she's reading something in a book
about dance in a romantic century

he's circling closer
nonchalant slow steps
on his toes
an insinuation whose eyes
are glancing elsewhere

this is coincidence
a pirouette from out of nowhere
she has closed the book
chapter ended
the dance is playing in her eyes
she doesn't see him stepping close

she pictures an arm held out
to hold her hand
rises to her feet
a curtsey
a responding bow
half-step into a romantic scene

he circles further out
away from her
he only saw her
from the corner of his eye
she didn't see him there at all

Musical Themes

he circles again
circles far away
doesn't see her anymore
she stops dancing
the reel that filled her head
has ended she

opens her eyes wide
and she can see a man in the distance
he's dancing around another reader
but he seems not to have noticed
not really

2002

dangerous decor

there's a TV against a wall
a sound box perching up on top
when I look around I see
the dregs of recent days
curling up in each stray corner

my table is invisible beneath paper
and the futon wears those clothes of mine
that are waiting for an ironing
when the cleaner comes
on Friday in a week or so

sometimes at night
I make the music cry out loud
so I can dance alone
in the spaces left upon the carpet beige
under a faded light from the weak-watt globes
that hardly shine enough
to show me where my feet should go
so I don't stumble or maybe fall

even in my small domain there's danger
of a stumble or a fall
if I'm careless or unwary
when the music cries
and I'm dancing
all alone

May 2000

especially with music

it's only my fingers made gentle
to run across your skin
in an exploration where
cupping the curve of your face
is a fresh journey
every time I touch you

I can't help it
especially when there is music
your body is all I know how to play
and I need to stroke you
with the whole of my hand
or my fingertips

what else do lovers do
when they are sitting quietly
I really don't know
but these hands of mine
have a need to move over you
and to find where you are

perhaps it's because you don't stop me
or that I can see you enjoy
these small touches
from the rhythm of your breathing
the closing of your eyes
and the special smile
that weakens me with pleasure

April 2000

in song and silence

She said

> *Why do you do that?*

He asked:

> *What is it I do?*

She said:

> *You sing.*
> *I only met you this evening,*
> *but it seems to me that you sing*
> *all the time. Under your breath,*
> *whenever we stop speaking.*
>
> *Why do you do that?*

He thought:

> *Do I?*

Mumbled:

> *Well, I don't know, do I sing that much?*
> *To fill the spaces?*

Disconcerted, he sat in thought,
oblivious
to a growing silence.

in the rehearsal room

in the corner of the room
she's set up a kind of mobile stage
with a keyboard and a microphone
song passages on a music stand
the foot pedal below
waiting for a touch

the black-vinyl chair
is almost ready to sing now
and all that's needed is
no
there it is now
just arrived
the staccato beat of raindrops on tin
is the applause she needs
to start the show

a few notes on the keyboard
before she sings…

~

I listen from the stalls
a small bed against the facing wall
in this rehearsal room

it's like a concert played for one
or two
and the dog and I
are appreciative
it's not every day
we hear her play
she's so often on the road
to a cafe
or a pub
to private functions
where neither of us can attend
uninvited

so we soak it all up
take her in
and know each song
has a private side
she only shares with us
on a night like this
with the rain applauding from the roof
the fire burning bright
and a bed against the wall
of this rehearsal room

her music surrounds us

~

it's time to get ready

I can see the professional look emerge
and the assumption
of some distance

she has sorted out
the music for tonight
now packing equipment in the van
keyboard and p.a.
stands and mikes
and music books
all tuck away in places familiar

back to the room to change
black pants
black top
the elegance of formal darkness suits
because tonight
she's set for business
playing for pay is no amateur affair
and attention to detail
is a step towards the next job
and another pay

Musical Themes

mascara in general
this brush in particular
is a recalcitrant tool to use
as an aid for the enhancement
of beauty

it layers in lumps and
to my eyes
is a shading un-needed
but takes just one place in a pantheon
of eye-liner and blush
even a colour to darken the lightness
of lips I adore
as they are
just as they are
as she is

but I know nothing of these things
and stay quiet with my thoughts
while she musses her hair
with a customised wax
then
standing above me -
a cheat in big heels -
I have to look up and reach higher
to kiss her goodnight
and
good luck
all the best
slay them all at their tables tonight
with your voice
and these wonderful songs you've rehearsed
here before us
me and the dog
and the rain on the roof

I'll do the dishes
I'll keep the fire alive
and we'll wait for you
to come home

late shift and the lonely bull

do you remember 'the lonely bull'
a slow brassy number
done by some ensemble from Mexico
they were popular for awhile

I don't remember that is
not really
but these half dozen trumpet notes
are playing
over and over in my head
sort of soothing
almost nuisance
and I'm sure they come
from that band
and that tune
nearly forty years ago

it's late
I'm supposed to be working
ba-da-dada-da dada   da-da-da
a chorus without words
the way some girl vocalists can do
it's haunting
beautiful I suppose
playing in the back of things
lonely and tugging sad

it's late

May 2002

Art

creation study

he is positioned to catch good light
on his back with one leg held straight
the other bent upwards

the temperature is a little less than warm
and the hairs of his legs and arms and stomach
have stiffened slightly
noticeably
as an easel
brushes and colours are readied

he is quite still
with eyes seeming focused
towards a far corner of the ceiling
or beyond

but in truth the gaze ends
only a short distance into the air before him
at a place where he has conjured
a lined page from inside his mind
and an image of his hand holding a pen
in the act of writing verse
about an artist and her model

he cannot think perfectly in this medium
an error needs erasure
by a hand raised and finger pointed
to stroke mistake away

the impression caught on canvas
is a study of stillness
in the act of correcting creation

July 2001

curves add character

she draws big bottomed women
in a class of fifteen.
She says that
curves add character.

I can't draw, but my hand can trace
the curve of her back.
Lying in my arms I see
that she has character.

She drew my face on a kitchen pot.
When I asked her why
she said, you know
that curves add character.

March 2001

dress sense

Published in e-zine ~ (the poetry) Worm 12

darling it's magnificent
what a creation
beautiful colours and so stylish
I simply love it

it's only when I look a little closer
that a few small things make me wonder

that seam threaded across the bust
reminds me just a tiny bit of something
I saw several seasons ago I think
it perhaps a little too early
to try to bring that back
don't you agree?
less classic than cliché really
no?

the back now
just a tiny bit higher to offset
the plunge of the front
less filigree for the straps
you don't see it?
of course dear I understand
lord knows through the years I've seen
several successful variations
yours may work

oh
the hem

too lacy too many frills
any elegance is lost in over-pretty patterns
I really think it should go
for the good of the creation
you wouldn't want to spoil
all the wonderful work you've put into it
would you?

well just give it a little more thought dear
I'm sure it will be perfect

such a clever girl
if only she would listen

May 2001

essentially enigma

i will draw you in a dervish
swirl from pallet onto paper
cream and dimple hungry
for the shape and hue emergence
of you
from rapid dabs and strokes
by brushes coarse for vital shape
and background fine for definition
of the porous contour detail hid
inside the mystery of your face

I whirl around unsteadied
by your eyes brown on the canvas
watching every line and mark I make
to fill demanding empty spaces
like a judgment needing eyebrows
and the shape of mouth to better cast
a verdict on my fever rush of colours
stroked in the flurried brightness
of deluded acts to catch what is
essentially enigma

2001

Frank Prem

fashion cleanser

every monday it's wet surfaces
on knees with washing cloth
and liquid cleanser

bathrooms and kitchen
wipe down chairs and vacuum
some days the refrigerator

we don't often say much past
hello how are you
but once she said:

> *this is no be forever Frenk*
> *is for my children*
> *is not what I do for all my life*
>
> *I was maker of feshion clothes*
> *feshion in Warsaw before ten year ago*
> *I come here to live*
>
> *aoh*
> *in show my girls wear gold tiara and dress*
> *you know*
> *long dress*
> *with here cut so and   so*
> *walk little bit like this . . .*
>
> *in my heart still is designer*
> *but here*
> *must work something*
> *for money*
>
> *is not feshion but is work*
>
> *I would one day like be artist again*
>
> *artist yes*
>
> *Frenk*
> *where you want me put you poem pages*

June 2001

ink, pastel and water

use firm strokes of the pen
to draw the outline
i was taught by the wise
that feints and multiple strokes
are for the uncommitted and the unsure
so if you mean to draw
draw as if you mean it

it's important to get the initial draft right
but there is room for limited extra lines
if they add texture or structure
even if they are to be painted out
or subdued by colour into insignificance
at some later stage

the sketch must be capable of standing
quite alone and without colour
complete in its own right so that
when you enter the studio to catch
the very first glimpse you should sense
the options being presented

pastel lends the softness of powder
like virgin snow it has depth without resistance
and a capacity for suggestion
with which the hand may judge the pressure
or the sensitivity that is required
through the stress and direction
exercised by fingertips

wash the work with waving strokes
of water from a fine brush that will
set in final place the colours but beware
this step may bring you undone
the shades you chose may alter under water
and your vision may be gone
wash on however until the finish
and let us see the outcome that emerges
from the application of your craft

don't forget to sign your name and mark
so none forget that you
were the creator

July 2000

iris and orchid

iris and orchid
together on a page you drew
shapes and added colour

nothing brings you back
so much as sketches
left behind

blue and purple iris
orchid yellow

i can find no perfume
in pen and pastel

January 2001

male nude

don't linger on his body long

men have ways to distract you
from seeing age and lines
by using posture and position
to make themselves the star
when they're only another subject

concentrate inside his eyes
that's where they often hide
and if you can catch the hint
of hesitation or fear of ridicule
you have him by the heart

build his body to surround it

arrogance and thinning hair
broken veins on upturned nose
a hint of cataracts denied

built muscles under paper skin
rigid chest with whisps of grey
flaccid length between stick legs

reflected sheen on fragile thighs
a buttock sag seen from behind
varicosity in a duck-egg blue

concentrate inside his eyes
when you have him by the heart
his body builds around it

he is only another subject

May 2001

modest art

it's only modest art we share
between us
you and i in little statements
with pen and ink and running water colour
streaking over empty pages
that are waiting for a mark
to hold on to the place or time
in a record of what we have done
or seen

i am writing words to fill the spaces
around your pictures like a framing border
to the images you leave for me to find
inside a postal tube upon my doorstep
as an inconspicuous surprise
that triggers my secret smile
while introducing new and novel ways
to write another line or two for you
to make you warm and wonder
about the picture you might brush and stroke
to mail me in a modest way
a little of the art we share
between us

July 2000

Frank Prem

painted daybreak

appeared in Map of Austin poetry E-zine #193-1 July 2001

the clouds are all van gogh waves
breaking on an upside-down blue sea
captured in a glow of light-gold
then fading grey into the western horizon

counted shapes in a winter-empty tree
are six black crows cawing
at a moment that needs reflection on canvas

I am no vincent
only a word-man
left to scribble awe
on tattered note book paper
from the middle of the road
at the raising of a painted daybreak

June 2001

Art

permootations of light and shade

Appeared in: Dancing Shadows: An anthology by members of the Fellowship of Australian Writers (F.A.W.) : Bayside Writers Group, 2002 - 2003" Melbourne, Australia

cows are one dimensional

she said

*or at least
black cows are
when you see them
against a hill or a solid background*

*it's because there is no light
or shade
just black
so it is impossible to sense depth*

*you always need light and shade
to have depth
in your cows*

she said

June 2002

picture on a wall

pastelled into a picture-frame is landscape
slow blowing a breath of heated wind through my hair
underneath a eucalyptus branch showing bark
as fine as paper done in greys and reds
and the brown map of cicatrising insect trailings

into mountain shapes faded by a hazy distance
like dim colour-clouds filtering the vision
of sky baking down beneath the summer
of a gully eaten out in some long past flood
that grew from an innocent original intention
to settle down the dust that I can taste
in billowed drifts of coated grit
from sandy topsoil loosely shaded on a foreground

sun that makes me squint-eyed
against the glare
of barren places I have seen and trodden
with the peculiar thirst
brought on by empty spaces
where in the constant burn
of drying loneliness
a drink of even tepid swilling-water
is like a step
along the road to heaven
in drooping shade
that's hanging just as thinly
as the paper on a cigarette
rolled between the softened curl of fingers
from a handful wisp of drifted smoke
rising up in studied contemplation
of some old picture on a wall

April 2001

portraiture

a photographic likeness is not necessary
although
some of you may become
commendably skilled
at such replication over time

think however about the ways
it is possible to recognise a person

your mother   your child   your lover

in silhouette   by profile   from behind

a slump of the shoulders
or the bending of spine in a way
that fixes unmistakably in your mind
characteristic curves and lines

these contain the personality
of your portrait
and of yourself
the artist

do not waste the breath
of your living model
in the lifelessness of an instamatic image

May 2001

sculpting in spanish

for some reason it is Spanish

starting with a rattle
away in the depths of the house
an electrical refrigerator-hum drifts
room by room
gathering the blunted sounds
of preparations from the workshop,
and the deep-fried odour
of paraffin on the boil in the kitchen
but fading almost before it reaches awareness

I sense you scraping
the narrow chisel in your hands
moulding from the soft warmth
shapes that will be poured tomorrow
wax to bronze

my mind offers an accompaniment
of flamenco castanets
stamping feet
whispered moans of passion and ecstasy
unintelligible but clearly formed
to add soul to your creation

tonight your shapes are Spanish

May 2002

sing calligraphy

i'm waiting for the song the song
of words to fill my mouth
with shapes to scratch on paper
for you to read and hear inside
your head

please sing for me

i can't hear the sounds that flow
out of my pen and make a mark
where i have been
until you tell me what you read
on the page that i gave you

it's a strange sound

these songs are a calligraphy of sorts
about you and me and love sometimes
but i wonder if i really mean it and you ask
if it's only the structure of a word or two
or is it the sound of my heart coming out
in the only way i know how to say things
that aren't clumsy mumblings
but look like elegance on paper

how much is real?

i hope the song the song
when it comes into my mouth
and finds it's way into a shape
i can scratch on paper
is a sound you can hear inside and read
and sing for me

clear notes and truth

September 2000

sky points

someone has time on their hands I think

a lot of time

since this morning when I first looked
the vast acreage of the sky
has been imperfectly converted to canvas
and pointillised with spots of cloud
white dots on blue
over the whole expanse

three parallel curving lines
in the south-east corner
the artists signature

May 2002

summer parchment

the summer parchment is beneath my feet
and I am writing you a letter

from the stilled wetness
that is no longer stream or creek
algae chords a trail of texture
forming words to etch with the spiked point
of a stick broken clear from its skin
to show itself in dull brown
and brittle nakedness

the language of a lone cicada
is the constant undertone
of distant muttering that emphasises
silence and intrusion
when listening hard reveals only futility
inside a sucking wave of dried heat
that inhales all hinted life
but the sound of breathing

bled from the sun the page
is a stained and squinting yellow
flecked with the dirty green of moss
gone dry beside pallid lichens
and the littered decay of trees
no longer pointing body and soul
to a sky whose only mercy
is the promise of coolness in the night

I will blot the words with dust
raised on a breeze of fool illusion
turning round and around
like a child at play and toying
at the idea of a break
outside the monotony of heat
and the dry of thirsting days

Frank Prem

I will sign with the sagging leaves
that reach down
prepared to fall
to the summer parchment beneath my feet

as I am writing you

February 2001

Art

yellow roses

featured in OZpoet Treasures from the Board January 2001.
'Manifold' poetry magazine (UK) 'Roses' competition, November 2001:
Equal third place

we bought the yellow roses
with a blush of red
at the end of budding petals
to make a sketchbook picture
to remember

you plucked leaves away from stems
and placed them tall inside a pitcher
with a yellow rose facing each direction
but you didn't get to draw them
because love fell in the way
and made a small distraction

in the morning they were opened
a little fuller in flower and soft perfume

there's no picture in the sketchbook
but i think that i'll remember
the blushing red of yellow roses
that never made a picture

June 2000

The Magic of Writing

poet in the rubble (of 9/11)

we misplaced a tiny voice today
I used to read him on the line
before the rubble closed him down
and I may not see his thoughts again
may not read the things he has to say
about New York and the view
from the 100th floor across Manhattan
and its statue

I haven't always paid attention
sometimes I've passed him by
too busy in my head to read
the outpouring of his verse
but I knew that he was there
penning words
on a scrap of paper or on a screen
to share them with a world
where I am a neighbour and a friend
and a loser now

we misplaced another voice today
has anybody heard from Colin
beneath the rubble?

September 2001

poetry on saturdays

The poets of the world are gathered - Saturday,
they're queueing up to caress
the metal microphone.
The Dan is as full as any time I've seen it.
the place is like a magnet for the found
and the unknown,

and they're in a line,
drawn upon the chalkboard,
waiting for their name to be declared.
A hundred eyes are looking up,
gazing on the speaker,
waiting for another soul to be shown,
and to be read.

It's a movement through the naked,
bared emotions,
of something in a life
that we can all appreciate,
because each of us
has travelled rocky pathways
to capture these small moments,
small moving moments to relate,

and, to read them, to read to *you*,
who listen,
with your hearts open wide
to every meaning found.

It's for you we touch
the things we've never spoken,
and turn them into written words . . .

try to make some sound.

The Magic of Writing

The poets of the world all gather, Saturday,
in the sound-wired room,
beyond the 100 Guinness bar.
The Dan is the place
of spoken word performance,
every one that fronts the microphone's a star.

And once in a while, once in a while,
 just once in a blind, blue moon,
someone will rise right up
and hold you in his hands,
as you listen to the stories,
the hurting, breaking stories,
as you listen to the deep, inside that man.

Then, somehow, you know
that you've been changed.
there's something that's altered,
in the air, just there.
Something that's been moved inside,
it's something like the truth,
or a thing that's swept and picked you up, taken you somewhere.

There's no way you can ignore it,
no doorway to escape,
he's whispered into your hidden place, i
nsinuated right inside.
Those words on you, are a red, raw mark,
and there's nowhere left to run, and just no place that you can hide.

In the Dan O'Connell, the spoken word place,
the poets of the world gather, every Saturday.
The Dan's the place to hear words out loud,
come and listen, come and hear,
come and stay,

on a Dan O'Connell, poetry Saturday.

July 1999

Frank Prem

reading modern poets

Appeared in PK List Featured Poets, December 2000

I'm reading some modern poets
because somebody said I should
or perhaps it's more true
to say that I'm glancing at them
peering through their lives
and between their verses

I really don't care for poetry

but maybe there's an interest
in the reasons why
they wrote this line or that
(if someone's done an analysis)

or even better if they can tell me
what the writer was all about
in the middle of that night when
he or she should have been sleeping
instead of burning candles
and putting words around
a spark or a flame
before it sputtered or went out
or simply faded from mind
the way I find my thoughts do

but I really don't care for poetry

and I hope they aren't just dull and boring
people not fitted out for anything better
than a life by pen and ink
and fluffy words that try to sidestep
each obvious cliché and overworking
of tired rhyme

The Magic of Writing

I wonder if they read their poems in bar-rooms
to check the metre and the flow
under a half-spot light
with a home-made lectern
that would make their pages fall down
all across the stage in the middle of a verse

and did they have an audience that listened
to what they said instead of only hearing
bursting Guinness bubbles
or laughing out loud
at the drunk that always sits over there
on poetry days
propped up in the corner
and reciting Shakespeare
from the vaults of a thespian youth
and taking all my bows if there's any clapping

I'm reading some modern poets
but I really don't care for poetry
all that much

June 2000

rhymer

the rhymer finds a corner spot
a seat under the window
with the light coming in behind him
casts an eye around the room
a hotel where open readings are
part of every Saturday for the committed
the persistent and the lonely

needs a line to get him going
perhaps a trick to force a smile
with hinted double meaning
and a killer rhythmic pulse
delivered with a pause of expectation
and an emphasis on the last line
of the final clinching stanza

but nothing much is happening
try another beer to make a bubble of thought
three o'clock is past and free-versers
with their grubby little words in hand
are making contented conversation

a rhymer going home unread
on the corner at the traffic lights
he's stopped and stalled and waiting
for a line or two that will sing out loud
in the room of streaming window light
illuminating an empty page
that he somehow left behind him

April 2001

supportive analysis

I want him to read the words
and he will
at a price

he is a hard man
a pedant
one who knows what he likes and will say so
then in a follow-up note
advise me of my errors

punctuation
grammar
misinterpretation of natural phenomena

he wants to be unstinting
in his support
to be a help
to make each expression correct
but seems always unsatisfied

if the words
were his own
it would be different

February 2002

tell them anything

you think you've got them sussed
tell them anything you want
but they can always pick
the one from the heart
and they go quiet
don't say much
focus on the ground
don't want to see you in the eyes

tell em anything you like
make up a story
throwing in all the frills
but they can check you out
from a tone of voice
when you're telling them how it is

there's a silence
and a fixed soft gaze
somewhere across your shoulder

January 2001

The Magic of Writing

tell you a story

listen son
I'm getting on a bit now
and I'm afraid I'm going to die ignorant
there are so many things
I always wanted to know
things I wanted to ask my father
things about his father
but you know
we never had that many moments

when we came to this country
both of us had young families
and we had to work
before that it was chaos

in the years after the war ended
the only times we'd touch on these things
was with friends or family
around to celebrate an occasion
or to visit
and there was hardly a chance
to go into all of it then

there's no-one left
now the old man is dead
I am the last
there isn't anyone to ask
anyone that remembers

I need to tell you a story
from when I was a young man
not much more than a boy really . . .

October 2001

teller of small tales

Just a teller of (small) tales
Singer of tuneless songs
User of words in little ways
Tiny thoughts and aching longs.

Take you away on a little ride
A carnival of expression
Walk with me just a little way
Sit back, enjoy the session.

July 1998

The Magic of Writing

telling the come-what-may

Published in The Brown Critique (India) July - October 2001

and you who have the words must speak
for those of us who stammer with our tongues
tied into swollen knots of mumbles
rising red upon
our faces straining
from the urgent need to say
what we have done and what has happened
where we have journeyed and to understand
what it may mean

you must speak us into stories so the world
will feel the presence of another minor place
and the events that pass in lifetimes
spent outside the glare of fame or fortune
or attention
are shouted loudly in a relief
that is finally overflowing
it is you who have the gift
and you must give us life
inside your words

for we are forgotten into non-existence
by the weariness
of reluctant footsteps grounded newly
on a morning
when to rise is not to celebrate
but to brace against
the burdens and the calls
that stretch us almost
past the place
of holding on to hope and comfort
yet knowing that
as each day holds a pain too close
another may inspire

so tell us to the world
without the treachery of stutter
by listening our truths
into your open phrases of translation
that flow like a strike of meaning
into heads and minds
removed from feeling warmth
out of ordinary moments in ordinary lives
and normal suburbs
full of mortgage houses and desperation
as stakeholder
in our pathetic come-what-may

you who have the words must write
to tell them all our stories
you must tell of us
in the shapes and paragraphs
of spoken pictures
you must tell of us
in all our come-what-may

February 2001

the age of poetry

I read The Age each Saturday.
The Age.
Such an important newspaper,
conveying words to the middle-class informed.

I read the Arts sections and the Book Reviews,
invariably featuring a latest offering or two from poets,
discussed and commented on by fellow poets,
commending each scintillating stanza
to the literate reader
in a commanding and authorative voice.

> *This is written art. Everyone must buy,*
> *read or listen*
> *to this work from another exemplar*
> *of modern bohemia.*

Then, I read the featured poem of the week,
and think about buying or borrowing
crime fiction.

May 2001

the letter nothing

I was thinking of writing
a letter to someone to give them some news
but I decided not
there's no news to tell
and no-one to tell it to

I watch as my keystrokes form
like ink on a page that is really a screen
I pretend that it's more
enough to feel real
black grown on blue

this must be a letter
it must be a letter penned for myself
pressing to make words
pressed hard to think
a little left justified

I was thinking of writing
but there's nothing ...

September 2001

the storyteller

Appeared in PK List Featured Poets, December 2000

Open my hands
Give you roses
Open my hands
Give you sun.

I open my hands
You see worlds in their palms
Without you believing
There is none.

Open my hands
Walk the valleys
Open my hands
Climb the hills.

If I open my hands
To new worlds and magic charms
They came there
By your will!

Open my hands
Fight the battles
Open my hands
Sail the seas.

If I open my hands
Into tempest or calm
We two may sail
As we please.

Open my arms
Taste a promise
Open my arms
Kiss your dreams.

If I open my arms,
Yes, if I open my arms
To tell you my stories
Your dream is as real as it seems.

July 1998

thereafter

I whispered for the first time

    I am a poet

she did not hear
and I took a moment to reflect
to gaze over images
I have seen in my mind
stories that have unfolded before me
tableaux that play out in my mind
after I close my eyes at night
to sleep

and I said again
louder

    I am a poet

she was silent for a heartbeat . . .
two
replied to me

    I know
    I have listened to the sound
    of your breathing

thereafter I was

2003

words and music

me
well I'd rather do music
I think it's unfair
to be stuck with playing smart-arse
around a paltry bunch of words and mark you
they're mostly the exact same collection
of baubles of babble you'll see on any dog-ear
used over and over again
for the sake of one more new sentence structure
or some fool of an idea that just needs to be written
so people can tell if it really fell in the forest
or not
even if it was just the one hand clapping
or pen penning
or whatever but it has to be the music for me
that rise and fall of melody and song
I'm going around and humming
or singing something all the time
you know doing a tune that nobody
ever heard before
I can make it sound all right too
a very rich timbre I have
when I hum away to myself
melodic
and if I could write just one of them down
I'd make a fortune for sure
because somebody would be wanting
to make a record and offer me ongoing royalties
but that of course is where they fail
because there appears to be no way
to write these things
these wretched words let me down
at the critical juncture
and I can do nothing but scratch
terse notes
to no-one in particular
bemoaning my fate
mostly non-harmoniously

The Magic of Writing

words
damned rubbish in my view
no good for saying any bloody thing
no use for music

August 2002

working on a phrase

i used a foreign phrase in a poem I wrote
took it home for checking with my ma and pa

mama said

>   *you shouldn't talk like that*
>   *it isn't right to spread such things around*
>   *and when she told me what it meant*

I said

>   *ok, I'll remove it*

papa took the verse aside for awhile
to study in the evening quiet
he said

>   *goodnight to all I'm going to bed*
>   *by the way son I think*
>   *you can keep the phrase*
>   *croatian men talk like that a lot*

I said

>   *ok, I'll keep it in the poem*
>   *and let the skippi's work it out if they can*

let them work it out if they can

July 2001

The Magic of Writing

writing and saying almost anything

some people can write about
almost any little thing
anything that comes to eye and mind
in a pattern or a shape that bears translation
into words that draw small pictures
like any painting hanging up
on any plaster wall
with a light pointing down to make a highlight perhaps
out of the petals of a red red rose
as liquid as blood
in the middle of a vase accommodating
a still life
that moves the watcher to another place
where the perfume wafts to fill the senses
and begin another crazy round of illusion

some people can say almost any little thing
anything sharp to draw a breath or gasp
sometimes bringing wit right into the play
but often only tiny prickle barbs
that needle like a finger poked into a scratch
or a sore that is threatening to open up
and pour out it's heart in a red red bleeding
in the middle of attempting to escape a still life
and relocate it to some better place
where words can draw moving pictures
and waft to fill the senses with crazy illusions

July 2000

advice

So what are you, son,
a writer,
or a mess with a pen,
waiting for a scribble to impress itself
from your pen to the page?

There's only three things can happen,
you know?
You're going to write it down
by making your mind get to work
and dragging words out of your head,
instead of sitting on your arse bleating at me.
Or, somebody else is going to write it,
and you'll come around here,
sitting on your arse and bleating again.
Or it won't happen at all,
and guess where you'll be?

Go on and get out of here.
Don't come back
when you think you've got something to say.
If it's worth hearing
I'll buy it in a bookshop.

Sooner or later.

July 2001

april moon

all through the cooler nights of April
I wrote my songs and stories

pausing only
for moments taken
to gaze into
the pallid mystery
of a poets' moon
that shone
sometimes a feeble glow
sometimes hardly present
yet at other times
a gold balloon
abreast of the horizon
at first rising

I wrote down almost half
of everything I ever knew

penned to illuminate
and clarify
to obfuscate
and to destroy
I wielded this pen of mine
to make the necessary
private admissions
reveal myself in unguarded words
and personalised glittering symbols
the shaman of slippery words
with his onion staff
unpeeled

and I sang and sang
while the moon went past

night after night
as it cooled
I sang slower
sang quietly
kept voice within the sound
until at last
it was hardly more
than a whisper
that could have been the breeze
I felt
ruffling the coat
that I wear long
as talisman
and to kiss this
the moon of poets
goodbye
for she is gone and I
am almost
done in
by the cool of April nights

the songs
and all the stories

are etched deep into the paper
no longer secret words
nor enigmatic
merely a kind of historical accounting
for the poet moon that was

I abhor the coming
silence

April 2003

capturing magic

and the pulsing starts again
a coursing through veins
he can feel
like a pump pushing energy
and urgency

he fidgets
looks about
tries to think of a start

come on come on

an opening line
to set him on the road

just a thought that will let him write
a thought that will make him

he can lose himself in that first few words
tapped up on the screen
let go deep
into the evolution
and formation
of a story

he doesn't know why it came
about the road it took
doesn't think about where it might go
where he will travel

isn't worried about the ending
before the middle is done
until he can see what it will look like
the shape
the feel
the way he thinks it might sound
if he spoke it aloud
where do the rhythms fall
where is the beat

does it sing itself inside his head
conclude with that familiar gentle touch
that reaches back
to kiss the opening idea
then rings a bell inside his head
for hours to come

maybe he's nailed one
he might have caught it
in his mind
and turned it into black and white
on paper
so that anyone can see
a small way inside his head
or readily believe
that it was always this way
it is so real
they must have lived it
in a dream of another life

and maybe that's so
he's just the medium
the writer

how could he presume to know
how magic is done

2003

composition

his fingers move across the keys
to put words on a page
like the pressing of chords
to shape a spoken music
that will carry
his reader away
lost for awhile inside the little story-tales
set somewhere between the pounding
of drama
and the tinkle of love
softly played in words damaged
by a narration
that does not master the language well
perhaps from a foreign land
broken english and musical speech
deficient but done as well as he is able

it is always a solo
but he tries to convey an orchestration
of the life that he leads
by writing it for you
speaking of places and moments
of the things he sees
through tiny sonatas in a stanza form
with variations
moving from thought
through fingers
to paper
passed to you for inspection
to pronounce what you read and felt
did he craft a good story
does the music of his words
resound inside your head
after he has left you

2002

days of affirmation

some days
when the sky is a perfect deep blue
and the clouds mere scatters of light fluff

days when the myriad branches
of the eucalypt
are clear and the leaf clusters moving
in the wind
are vivid   offering both depth
and perspective
adding texture to the small corner of outlook
obtainable from the back yard

on those days I am glad to be a poet

December 2001

dot point poetry

words get in the way of writing sometimes
phrases reduce to asterisks and arrows
poetry is the price i offer up
for final drafts and deadlines
and pentameter is taking a long road home

so many things to say in a day
that's putting bread on the table
to eat in the evening if i'm still awake

every morning set the clock to call
in the middle of the dream i'm weaving
for a page of verse

i might have sung it for some listener
but the chirrup call distorted
now it's faded and it's gone
away from any of the places
i know how to reach

this is not the way i saw things when i started
nothing like the writer in my head
everything is words and paragraphs
instead of stanzas filled with couplets
or free verse resonating

it's not a way to keep fires stoked
more like a dulling
in the embers of something
that might have been
if i wasn't lost in projects and reports
and the executive sum
of rising recommendations

the poetry is dying
while the dot points pack a punch
but somehow that doesn't seem to be
correctly ascending order

July 2000

joe pretty-words

published in e-zine ~(the poetry) Worm 6

there's a fella
makes his home inside the small words
of reaching and touching and dance
on the footpaths and sidewalks
of sunshine and rain

tells stories to himself
and anyone can spare a second
if they want to

to listen

if they really want to

pretty words pretty words
like Christmas wrapping
and ribbons
or flowers left on a doorstep

he wants to reach out or to come inside your place
with his handful of pretty words

but who's going to listen can you tell me?
who's got the time
for touching and dancing and for reaching out?
nobody i know
no one that knows what they're doing
and anyway

what right does a joe with a pencil in his hand have
to grasp at a sky that flashes
with the twinkling of the masters
scattered across the spread of spoken words
in stanzas of movement and light?

The Magic of Writing

he's only a trier coming up cheap and fast
passing from our sight like a shooting star
to burn without leaving a smoke trail
or a mark on the ether or the sky
to point out the way he went

he's just like the rest of them
so who gives a damn huh?

> *shhh*
> *joe pretty-words is writing again*
> *wonder what it is this time*
>
> *anybody want to listen when he's done?*
>
> *anybody?*

May 2000

just a lifeline

this is just a lifeline.
It's only saying words.
Connection to the mainstream,
written, but unheard.
At least, the words are only spoken
in the recess of a mind
where the voice has lost the reason
and the sanity unwinds.

Just a lifeline.
Some kind of shouting hush.
A way of keeping company
in a crowded mental crush.
Murmurs on the paper,
and wandering monologues.
Lines of staggering hieroglyphs,
guard sentinels and dogs.

It's not important, like a heart attack,
there's no victim of the sounds.
Not even really punishment,
it's just releasing hounds.

October 1999

kinds of nothing

afternoon tv shows
even cartoons pass good time
textbooks on philosophy
don't hold attention
disaster shows on the news
reporters can't believe their eyes
I don't know what to think
I'm just spectating

watching raindrops fall
to my window from the sky
forming and falling
and then there's nothing
except another one coming down
in a pattern descending faster
than my understanding

so many kinds of nothing
I hardly notice the loss of hours
emptiness has hours to fill
and I'm trying
a sheet of white paper
disappears beneath a scribbled line
nothing worth saying and I'm the man
to do that job

2000

little stories

once upon a time
everybody hung on words
from poets, written in the journals and magazines.
Everybody from the far out back and bush
to the city streets.

>*What did The Banjo say?*
>*Did The Breaker write this week?*
>
>*I've done the things they tell*
>*and ridden just the way they say it.*

Once upon a time
almost everybody wrote a ballad or two.
Said it aloud, or sang at night
around the campfire to the horses and cattle,
or in parlours.

Stories, little stories,
about the sliprails, or the crops.
About no water from above,
about the dream of droving under stars,
from the confines of the town.

Once upon a time
everybody hung on words
come from the balladeers.
Almost no-one hears them now.

January 2001

long distance writer

the long distance writer
sets pen onto paper
no
he taps keys to make marks
on a fifteen inch screen
maybe seventeen
maybe smaller

the 's' key
isssss sssssticky
there's muck in the sssspacesssss
where commasssss might go
periodsssss and colonsssss
exclamationsssss
ssssso he digsssss out the 's' key
dissssplacesssss three hairs
a paperclip
two fluffballsssss
and a golden-brown crumb
from the bun he ate here
not more than a week ago

replacessssssssssss the 's'
with a firm prod
and a tes-s-s-t run
to see it's all working
and ready to roll

the long distance writer
interrupts his thought lines
he cannot think clear without coffee
to help the creation
of line breaks
and the rhythm and rhyme
in his head
are always in need of flat-white
as a lubricant

a moment please
the long distance writer
checks on his email
to see if there's a comment
from someone out there
some any old where
about the last piece he wrote
and submitted

he's only as good as he feels
and he feels quite strongly
that he's only as good
as the last piece
and the next
only as good
as the e-mailers tell him

the long distance writer
flexes his fingers
the coffee is already cold
ideas are fleeting and thin
but it's time to write something
so how should it start
maybe something about
writing a poem
from a distance
or the making of love
on a bright day of sunshine
the meeting of three people
at a party
and the things they said

perhaps better come back
later in the day
after lunch
after phone calls
after slow-reading the mail

The Magic of Writing

the long distance writer
is too busy to write now
he'll transfer a small verse
from keyboard to screen
at some other time
then post it for comment
to a place far away
that's as close as the button
that despatches messages to e-mail land
then wait till he hears some response
to assure he's still alive
still breathing
and valid

2014

man of flowers

when I see him there are flowers
drawn from his mind through an opened hand
and cast into the air

the scene is alive
but he and the flowers
are a still tableau

sometimes instead of flowers
I see stars

September 2001

marked - nothing to say

'I set my cup to leave a ring
to mark the places I have been'

not long ago
I would have eaten those opening lines
presenting themselves for consideration
while on the road
thinking about the way my coffee
overflows wherever I go
and how perhaps that is a device I use
for staking out my territory
the way that dogs do
or wild animals

that was yesterday
the words have been on my screen
since yesterday
and I don't want to save them
I don't want to shut them down
I want to use them in a story
in a poem
but I cannot write
I am a waste of opening lines

I miss the play
can't find a point
and I don't think I have a thing to say
that you would want to hear

I'm tracing with my finger round a coffee-ring
in the middle of my note-book page
surrounded by no words

there's not a thing to say
and not a thing to do
leave a mark of circle-brown
and move along

April 2002

no shortage

it should be straightforward
he said
to metaphorically reach your hand
into the streaming of consciousness
individual or collective
to pluck at will a single idea
examine it from all angles
and then to write it

if you are a writer
a poet
you should never want for material
never lack for the next piece
it is there for you
surrounding you in everything you do
waiting to be brought to life

July 2002

nothing much wrong with that

there was nothing wrong with that son
you held them in the palm
of your hands
and they were hanging on
to every word

you told them about the mundane things
that fill a life
and you made them listen

i think you could be a writer
i think you could do a book
they might like to read
when the cold is beating at their door
or before they close their eyes to sleep
in another night's repose

i really think they liked you
did you hear the way they laughed
when you mentioned something funny

there's nothing wrong with stories son
everybody has a handful or maybe more
and they want to know
that you've been there too
and that they're not alone
even in the silly little things that make a day
or an entire lifetime

you made them feel at home
and son
there's nothing much wrong
with that

June 2000

oncer

You want to fuck?

Don't worry,
time isn't a factor.
I'll make it work.

Come here.

Just remember,
this is a oncer.
Don't come crawling for remembrance
and recognition and repeats afterwards.

And no fucking poetry.

All right?

April 2003

Places and Locations

Places and Locations

a rural autumn

it's not often I get to use high beam
the cities and towns I inhabit
have street lights

tonight I'm driving out of town
it's autumn
the darkness falls easily
daylight is no longer supported

country driven miles pass easily
the landscape restricted
to roadside trees
white-lined bitumen
and guidepost reflectors

beyond my spearing light are paddocks
greening now
but topped with the yellow-brown
of last summer
easily forgotten on a journey through night

until a red glow in the distance
is not the moon rising
but a fire

until a bend in the road
is the twinkling brightness
of a city's lights
patterned and spread in small cool flame
across a kilometre square
of stripped crop
the burning attraction
of a rural metropolis of flame

for a moment I felt
I might have been on the doorstep
of melbourne
but it is only autumn
in the country

April 2002

an empty theatre

they laughed too hard
and laughed too long
in the breathing seat behind me

it wasn't really all that funny

I think they were
all of a particular age
maybe they don't get out much
or perhaps because the topic was religion
with a saccharine ordination
of safe humour

but I was slow to get the joke

I think next time I'll choose a movie
something that's a bomb
if anyone is going to do loud laughter
I think it ought to be me

and I prefer an empty theatre

June 2000

and so to work

the sun of morning east
casts tower shadows to drape Collins Street
in filter light across the backs
of scurry workers on pilgrimage
to their place of crusts and earnings
and the rituals of grinding
for another day

the tedium of noise and hurry again wakes
edifice and asphalt from slumber
with the metal grind and squeal of tram wheels
making right hand turns one minute late
according to the schedule posted
on the standing pillow of a potential passenger
too early from his bed
but still on time to meet the office
for a cup of coffee to arouse
admiration from the forty fourth floor

at the privilege of a view upon the south east
green of parks and suburban trees
flowing from the distant hills of the Dandenongs
along the wavering line of the muddy Yarra
passing beneath the oars of 'eights'
and bridges of determined traffic
glinting brightly at the green and empty courts
of the tennis centre
and the nine tracks of electric rail
bound inwards
to end finally in the shadows cast
beside a neighbouring tower
across the edge of Spring and Collins Streets
in the sun of morning east

and so to work

December 2000

at the armadillo

at the Armadillo
guitars hang in colours
on a wall shaded yellow and sunset
ukuleles are a light relief
of sky plus brown spaced
to make a little silent symmetry

in this homage to the desert
corrugated rainbow-iron
upholds a spotlight
for the mirror-ball twirler of reflections
to pout lipstick shapes that simmer
around the walls
in a slow-slow time
until we are half red kissed
by indicators of romance

the man in the hat
is aiming his saxophone at the cantina

and particularly at my table
he is striking home a long note
fired with his eyes tight closed
and blowing so hard
the iron sheets are a rattle
in the brassy breeze
of a cold barren night
but I am warm somehow

and my senorita is demanding
with a touch beneath the table
we should dance

June 2001

brisbane trees

the trees on Brisbane streets
are tall and broad.
They reach out to touch the sky.
Moreton Bay is awash in reds and blues
While Jacaranda purple-grey
tones sidewalks and back yards bathed
in suggestions of shade.

We've been to places where she was raised
to see everything is new
but still the way it was before.
Houses with wide, overhung verandahs,
the school and the old playgrounds.
It looks like those same old ladies
take mallets
to strike their sluggish coloured balls,
but a caravan of scruffy travellers
has a tent pitched by the croquet lawn
and there's no hoops lined up
no game to be played today.

I can see she's smiling
at the workings of recollection
but a little perplexed at the effect
of bringing it back to mind.
The things that are gone make gaps
touched with sadness of a loss.
Or it might be because they're still alive
to tease right into a tenderised soul.

Going back is a journey for the brave.

I wonder about the stories
hiding underneath those wide, curving eaves
and the familiarities pointed out to me.

There are things she hasn't had
a chance to tell. Time is short and almost over.
It may be that the roots from here
were the start of the life she's led,
or just a case of life happening to us all.

Brisbane trees don't seem to care, or know.

September 2000

Places and Locations

choir and accompaniment

> *the Grenfell Henry Lawson Festival of the Arts Verse Competition*
> *Winner of Section 2, Class 3 and awarded the statuette for best verse*
> *over all Class winners - June 2001.*

as the concert hall mutters quietly
in the act of settling
to the drone of strings
tightening and loosening for pitch and tone
from the front row
it is the evidence of character
that suggests itself
as much as the promise of music
and the rise and fall of harmony

the shining baldness of a conductor
with a virtuoso earring
catching the spotlight in flashes keeping time
to the sway of the tails of his suit coat
and the violence of a baton
wielding emphasis to his silent shouts
at players and choristers
leading and prompting each movement
to carol a birth that happened
a long time ago
in a place some way from here

young men and boys sing
while making entrance from the left
jostling vigorously to achieve
the exact place of rehearsal
from which they may present perfectly
the parts
practiced with relentless attention
before the tolerant the adoring and the stoic
for weeks beforehand

the bass men bow to each other
with every turn of the page
hearing all but standing a little apart
from the finesse of violin and cello
more comfortable in the proximity
of tympani and a bassoon

that puffs the cheeks and raises
the red eyebrows of its man
higher and higher
making large eyes that glance pointedly
sideways at sheet music tantalisingly close
to the edge of the range of vision

two violins are giggling between parts
something must have been said
but a look from the orchestra captain
is quite enough to quell
as the cellos saw away with gusto
and self-obsession while the kettle drums
acting as an entire percussion section
are managing sleigh bells and triangle
and proving themselves to be team players

the only brass to be heard
drowning out a rousing chorus
is the farting trombone
wielded with vigour by a red face
and uncomfortable belly that remind me instantly
of a cold glass of beer in the local pub

the female lead soloist protrudes her lips
in an 'O' to be proud of
her lipstick adorns and disappears
inside the mouth without change of colour
but the baritone wears dark and sinister shadows
in his ill fitting suit with the satin stripe
and sleeves that require a bent elbow
to allow the hands to move unhindered

the choir of course is young cherubim
with a beauty in the voices unbroken
and raised high in songs of praise
as deeper mature voices of support
thrum from the old-boys reassembled
for one more occasion and melody

if you close your eyes
in the front row to hear it
the rise and fall of music and harmony
is a transport to a heaven of angels
but if you prefer to watch
the melding of character and idiosyncrasy
is a richness in itself

December 2000

cockle bay 19/08/02

i

peter told me he'd dreamed I said that I hadn't come all this way to pay big money for flash restaurant food and of course that's exactly what I did say he thought that was eerie perhaps he knows me too well

ii

there is sunshine bathing cockle bay and the exhibition area

we are comparing the paved corzo-style expanse that leads to the waters of this little bay with the south-bank-on-the-yarra that we are more familiar with

an intricate set of water-paths spiral below ground level children and parents walk and play down and around then up all the time trying to avoid getting feet wet

a young girl-woman is cavorting with a child her pants up-turned from ankles to knees in an arresting fashion breasts tantalisingly close to exposure in a strapless top moving fluidly beneath flimsy materials as she risks over-balance and a revelatory experience while tottering on clumsy heels

disaster averted it is time to move on

iii

this bay hardly qualifies as scenic though designed to capture people and to facilitate movement

suspended roadways encircle and intrude their sound while skyscrapers form a solid and stark raised-perimeter to the east

nearby building facades are a touch *arse-end industrial* and all the colour seems to come from people passing

two girls - arm-in-arm and backpacks - strolling couples
      families   singles seagulls

we two stand in the centre hardly knowing where to turn

iv

this morning a plate-glass window from the fourth level
has been shattered outwards the area is cordoned-off
and the tasks of clean-up and replacement will take the
whole of the day diesel noise from the miniature cherry-
picker is a constant grumble of echoes across around and
enfolding communal areas and walkways

we have speculated the means and the cause of the
breakage this being the site for a conference on mental
health makes a half-joke and a half-relief to note that no
blood is evident in the detritus and debris of reflective
fragments of glass even though the jagged cavity above us
is approximately man-size

somebody said it was a bird

v

the diesel has stopped and the sun is disappearing I
have heard enough about the mental institutions of the
netherlands
the systems introduced into malmo fifteen years ago
the optimistic poverty of india and the basket-case that
remains romania

it is time to return to the hotel room for a nap before
official functions and the burble of social rounds that will
fill the evening

August 2002

easter parade weather

my mother told me

> *the weather*
> *always clings to fine until Easter has gone*
> *that's just the way it is*

there is always sun for the parade
of children on yellow-red decorated bicycles
draped flat-bed trucks swept clean
to hold some bearded fellow in a bush hat
fossicking for gold in a pan filled with sand
or a fiddle player and a dancing girl

the weather always holds until then
like a law that says there must be no rain
on the day of the parade

stalls are set each end of the street
to sell second hand collectibles
sterling silver chains   gemstone earrings
or leftovers from some failed garage sale
anything to bring a person with a dollar
tired of craning from the eighth row back
in the hope of seeing a float go by

perhaps a sausage
from the street-side barbecue
run by a deep sea fishing club
two hundred miles from any tide
or ocean beach
raising money for the next expedition
might tempt with the aroma of frying onions

Memorial Park is full of people hardly pausing
in the mad crush
of an ever-moving country market
overhung by a lazy drift of candle scent
that lingers on the baby clothes
lying next to wooden toys

home-made chocolates
and nondescript garden plants

it's grand to walk among these bodies
stopping every moment to handle craft
created by the woman drinking thermos tea
in a director's chair
and talking hard to the next stall-holder

my mother said

> *why don't you wander up*
> *take a look*
> *it's always fun*
> *this year will be a special one*

I don't think I'll go
maybe it's the weather
I don't know

April 2001

friday marching

police are at the lights
halting traffic
for a dishevelled line of twos and threes
mostly older and oddly formal
in long coats and small hats
with occasional children
like the misplacement of a Sunday

over the road to right-angle
past the few shops
and on towards the crossing

halted by the raising
of an arm shaded official blue
there is time to gaze
amongst them
in
around
and over
old ANZACs
in too-bright teeth
tottering dowagers
in mesh-veil hats

a younger man at the head
tall and skinny
bones and beard
carries a full-length lightweight cross
with measured steps
like the flag bearer at an olympic opening

little lies beyond he tentative crossing
of the railway tracks
now being negotiated by the leaders
that could cause them to march
against the Park Road traffic

Places and Locations

there is only a park and a cemetery
and the last of the meander-ers
a pink-frocked girl
skipping at the tail of the procession
on the arm of her gran
seems unaware of the purpose
mindful only of the direction

the police don't care

three vans have done their job
for this Friday morning
and move off at a crawl

and I
can proceed with my journey
and pull up at the bakery
to purchase the hot cross buns
that are my reason this morning

2002

gippsland traveller

there is hustle even at this early hour
on the way to leaving the city
lights glowing a red stoppage-time
as though each wishes to linger
in a peculiarly metropolitan form of farewell

passing flashes of red and white -
oddly spaced clumps of wildflowers -
signal the commencement of countryside
familiar from many journeys
and welcome markers of progress

the thought recurs that on one trip
he will stop to pick a single specimen
of each different flower that he passes
to take home as a gift   a token
he laughs at the idea of a journey
that would take days to complete
and a car overflowing with flowers
and scent

the freeway is divided by native flora
grown thick and tall to hide opposite lanes
a far cry from the autobahns of Germany
so many years ago
split by a mesmerizing blur of metal posts
winding through the Schwarzvald

follow   pass   follow
he plays tag with a hatchback
for fifty kilometers
no cruise control makes the speed variable
a nuisance and a game
the next car he gets will be a better model

there is a voice in his head   a hum
muttered to an unstable tune
in a guttural foreign tongue
perhaps not real words
but simple sounds

playing over and over

a lament to link unsung verses
and the passing of time

coffee at Yarragon
two hours before the first appointment
there is no need to reserve a room overnight
in the middle of the week
he always finds a vacancy
room fourteen smoking

on South Australian roads
they place special marker posts
black for the dead   orange for the injured
in Victoria it is wilting flowers
that are a coincidental aid to concentration
for the last leg into Traralgon

February 2002

lygon street

published in the Aabye's Baby Archive

Lygon Street is alive tonight
it's only a Thursday
but there's bodies everywhere
looking for a feed in the evening
I can't avoid a spruiker standing outside
with his best moustache and a menu
twitching at a chance to tempt me in
with a free red wine and something special
but I'm just walking now
taking in the scene and the people
scattered everywhere on a cold night
in the middle of July

every restaurant is tables and chairs
under a sidewalk-spread of umbrellas
embracing the buzz of a round of chatter
and the cosy hiss of portable gas heating
it almost makes me want to sit and place an order
from the Italian Lebanese Indian Malay place
that I'm passing now on this smorgasbord
street of multi-cultural cuisine
but I'm only sucking up the sounds
and taking in the scent
and wandering at my ease
once more up and down

Lygon Street

meteorology - a love story of melbourne

cool today you ruffle through my hair
just yesterday
you were the fire I had to hide from
but you have changed again

I wonder often about you and me
the mercurial
the reactive

I never make the running
I shy away to watch you
through all our day-by-days
I try to keep a balance
when you are warm you build me up
temperate you lead me higher
near to the planes of vertigo
and atmospheric tastes
that enervate my senses

but then you keep rising
seemingly insatiable
you steal my breath away
until I gasp in desperation
until I have to hide inside myself
and wait you back down and cooler
tomorrow
or some other day

I find you unpredictable
from burn
in an instant to ice and cold

I am confused to know
how best to bear the chill
you might blow over me
I place myself outside your reach
hide away
in artificial control
until I feel you smile

so intimate I have to come again
into your close embrace
let you hold me close
comfort me

some days you shine
a glory
wash your warm all over me
then you are most beautiful
I name you my Desiree
my journey
I travel you
through every day by day
from storm
to storm

December 2002

mcg (black and white and blues)

i can feel it with my hand on a wall
the MCG alive with rumbled dull thunder
vibrating through acres of concrete and brick
the first twenty thousand to gather
are trembling the foundations of this coliseum
we are early but the filling of the tiers
has begun

the reserve teams are the 'dew-kickers'
out on the field of play from lunchtime
in the role of lesser spectacle and time-filler
before the pre-match singing entertainment
and announcements
until the commencement of the main attraction

this stand is a babble for the big one
black and white plays navy blue
the place in front of us casually reserved
by a blanket spread the precise
posterior width of two men and a child
on a peeling wooden bench painted
the dull but distinctive shade of green
that is recognised universally as
'Members Only Seating'

my companions are here for a first time
it is all a new excitement but by half-time
we are losing
the boy is rocked halfway unconscious
from the thumping sound of so many goals scored
by players coloured black and white
and magpie
and the first grim consideration
of going home early has been raised
for we are shaded darkly glum
in the absence of any coherent defense
by the rabble
undeservedly wearing navy blue jumpers

I can see a thousand people in curving rows
on my right hand side
like so many background faces
in a crowd painting
white and pink and lacking feature
all craning forward for a better view

of the dasher wearing forty-three
who has the ball in hand
surely he can turn the game around

in the shaking crescendo rises
from the massed crowd speaking as one
to shout the statement
that he has fired through the goal
between defenders
leaving them looking as foolish
as small children
in an arena intended for occupation by adults
we may still be in the hunt
for this trophy game

the scoreboard at the last break informs
that we are some
seventy-five thousand representatives
of two teams engaged in peaceful battle
over all the long years since Federation
but we don't care
for our boys have hit the front
and we are screaming for them
to take the black and white apart
and leave only a cloud of floating feathers f
or their mascot to collect
when we are done with them

at the siren it is over and we are beaten
because we began playing as a team
far too late
but I can't be overwrought on a day like this

the tribes have done their battle
under the sun of tradition at the MCG
and we have cheered and called
until I am so hoarse that a croak
is all the comment I'm able to offer
while making our way to the football train
through a happily buzzing crowd that knows
this has been a good one

May 2001

Frank Prem

moorabbin airport, july 29, 2002

the setting of the sun pours paint
across the western sky
turns single engine aeroplanes
into avian silhouettes
gliding lower just above my head
on approach to landing
rising acutely to achieve departure
black streaks
suspended against the spread of orange

it is sundown at Moorabbin

the birds above the airfield
do not fall to earth
with the descent of evening
they flock and fly in lazy sweeps
across runways
without resort to traffic control
length to length
they rely on a visual approach
and seem not to require
the formal protocols of
see and be seen
hear and be heard

pelican flotilla   ibis solo
a wheeling phalanx of starlings   gulls

Moorabbin birds can find their way
around the airport terminus
they do not land on top of each other
as dusk descends
they do not crash   they do not die
from the absence of air-traffic control
after six o'clock
beyond the orange of sundown

July 2002

non-photographic south

this is not a photograph

the composition however
seems close to perfect
from the clarity
of near-focus volcanic brown scoria
larger than pebble   smaller than fist
to the symmetry of parallel pairs of lines
riding the brown over a middle-distance ridge
implying disappearance
after breasting the rise
then perfectly aligned reappearance
without a break visible to the eye
separating by cleft suburbs from bay
until the point of nothing
at the distant end of sight

this is not a photograph
just the current framing
of a way to travel south

January 2002

not better than this

    crump   *crump*

the sound of cars across the cobbles
of the pedestrian crossing

interrupted by a piercing squelch
and the monotone of a rapid-fire

    tuk-tuk-tuk-tuk

then silence
for a moment of stopped traffic
and a half a dozen noisy teenagers
spreading across the width of Charman Road
between railway station and post office

so much for a peaceful hour
in the shade of an umbrella
between the pages of a book

the coffee is tinged
with the smell of stale, burnt cooking fat
or vegetable oil wafted and lingering
from the damned takeaway
that's somewhere behind
god help the poor wretch
that carries home fish and chips
cooked in that muck tonight

    crump   *crump*

    squelch

    tuk-tuk-tuk-tuk

    silence

    smell

Places and Locations

it doesn't get much better
than this

April 2001

on charman road

charman Road people brace the wind aside
shoulder deeper within the layers
of doing what's necessary
ignore the favourable possibilities
of an inside table
to hunch over kerb-side latte
and primary smoke inhalation
raise their heads outside of coats
for minimal moments
that cause an icy tear to form
and trickle down
before being brushed by a rapid-fire hand
unfolded only briefly

it's cold enough for stoics
on Charman Road

hands in pockets
folded-over arms
red-and-white knuckle plastic grocery bags
trembling breath and body

hugging melee of one

god it's cold on Charman Road

July 2001

paradise falls

the waters of paradise
don't flow in the summer
but trickle in droplets
from the head of the falls

I have counted them down
on their journey
one drop at a time
until they dampened the moss
on the rocks at my feet
and were gone
to wherever the waters
of paradise go
when they have drifted
to ground

through the spare heated air
of a dry inland summer
that reduces the flow
down to droplets
that I counted one day
when I was a young man
with a bride on my arm
before we too
drifted to ground

April 2003

pebbling brown

a good straight wall
concrete cast

rend the brown mortar
smooth across the surface
to a height of four or five feet

set the scaffolding
and mount for the next level

and while the mortar is still sticky wet

      you   get the trowel . . .

and load it flat-surfaced
with brown pebbles
then with strength in that wrist
flick hard   really snap it
to fling those pebbles
onto the mortar
and they will stay there
snap and snap
flick and flick

that's how the wall will be done
that's how we do brown pebbling

October 2001

perhaps a long spring

the walls of this medical centre
are coated with brown pebble mix
from ground to the sixth level
where a walkway joins two buildings
via the mechanism of a substantial steel girder
painted white and featuring a small gap
between the girder itself
and the construction above

it must be spring
because apart from the warm sunshine
dashing clouds and lazy breeze
there is a sparrow clinging vertically
to the pebble mix at level two
with its mouth over-full
of construction material for a nest
struggling for a panted breath
before proceeding to hang vertically again
on the edge of the girder
and finally entering the gap with a flurry

too much flurry

the enthusiastic entrance of our young male
and perhaps new father
dislodges

feathers

dry grass ball

paper

three sticks

the grass ball and a feather float lightly
cross and recross in the air
then land either side of my feet
which are based firmly on ground
and adjacent to level one

the sparrow watches me for a moment
with what I fancy is a baleful eye
and I almost see the deep breath taken
before he flies off in another direction

some of us
might be in for a long spring
this year

October 2001

pink throb latte

the noise never quite succeeds here
in fading to background white
it is shaded by the pink and throb of night club
not the mannered brown of café

this is Chadstone
two hundred and thirty two retail outlets
and a myriad hustling bodies
almost blinding in a random agitation
of movement
it is here I have come
for a daily paper-and-coffee indulgence
dependent for success
on a dominance of the white over the pink

the food-court is in session
broad enough for perspective to play a role
in shrinking size if not numbers
as the eye scans to the distant edge
of the twitching tables that lie
between my bubble of hubbub
and the perimeter markings of
Indian take-away (roti wrap curries)
gourmet carvery
steakhouse grill
and home-made ice-creamery

the mass at rest before me crawls
seething in an incessant irritation
seated or upright
afoot or undulating
in the dis-coordinated breeze
that drives this shop-town community

each table grouping a micro-climate
of independence
working for the common purpose
of a retail hive
humming pallid
against the throb-pink
of latte and morning papers
that never quite recedes
to background white

July 2002

pink upon the avenue

the prunus trees are showing pink

it must have happened overnight

signs of change
unfolding down the avenue

it doesn't mean that winter is gone
bitter cold remains in control
but today there is no wind
sun has banished the idea of cloud
the bringers of both rain and storm
are at rest

already I can see settling dew
waiting for frost to form in the early hours
white and cold

the trees
dressed in pink bouquets -
are a beckoning for spring to return
to our avenue

July 2001

pleasure complex

in its way this seems almost
an industrial setting
stark and intense accommodation
for such simple pleasures

close your eyes
and listen

behind the surface echo and clamour
is a deeper constant
rushing water
surrounding
purposeful
the breeze you feel on your bare back
and arms
is moving as though funneled down a shaft
lightening the closeness of clammy humidity

now open
what do you see

you might expect aquatic blue to assert itself
but no
here it is a clinical white

roof and walls are white tiled
the grouting between each tile
a gash of black

the stairs are framed
in vivid white metal

spiraling tubes circle in descent
through a twisted mass of white fiberglass
in just five seconds
of forced and frenetic sliding
black rivets add the strength of contrast

living colour comes only from naked skin
and the harlequin costumes of bathers
queuing on the platform

awaiting their turn to use the apparatus
with its roaring slide
that fades to pitch
within a moment of entry
into the chasm

full length plate windows
show trees outside through steam
that clouds the glass
but the waving branches loaded with leaf
are overpowered
no match for the faded whiteness
of bursting clouds

white and wet
inside and out
it is perhaps as well
to immerse here

in the white dazzle
of this industrial pleasure complex
as it would be
to soak
in the pallid drizzle beyond the walls

April 2002

Places and Locations

pre-meeting at the grace darling, collingwood

there is a couple parked in the corner seat
a 'stubby' drinking man
and a long-tall-glass girl
he has a mobile stuck to his ear   talking
she has her legs tucked under her
on the brown leather settee
they don't stay long
got places to go

fellow on a stool has a red face glowing
and a glassy *three-kinds-of-stupid*
look on his face
that I can remember
from pub days back home
stupid in the morning until he gets
a heart starter
stupid around lunchtime
self-satisfied with the world
and stupid in the evening around closing
next stop coma

maybe every pub
everywhere
has its share of stupid red faces

the television is showing highlights
with the sound down
rain stopped play but the sound system
is still batting on

to an irregular bouncing strain of beat
doing nothing good
for the low pressure atmosphere of rain
above the Gabba cricket ground
that means we're all watching *yesterday*
with full attention

but the sound now
today
is reggae Collingwood

I know the woman at the table just behind me
she works in Health just across the road
our paths have crossed on some work-front
but I ignore her

this place is good to hold a meeting
or to wait
for the next one to happen
better -
god knows -
much better
than departmental corridors and enclosures
but I don't want to break my thoughts

she can get along without me

around the bar walls they have advertising
for the spring races
most hotels now are legal for a bet
and there's a thousand dollars going begging
for an open-mike maestro reading poetry

semi-finals already   on the fourteenth

nobody told me about it

I wish I'd known

guess I better have pre-meetings here
more often

I could learn so much

November 2001

quasi-cosmopolitan coffee

it's a quasi-cosmopolitan bohemia.
Long coffee on a sidewalk,
beneath umbrellas in the sun,
almost brings to mind the tables
of left-bank on the Seine
and berets at an angle, with colours
matching dollops on a pallet.

But the view lacks sufficient splendour.
A hundred cars can't move with the grace
of art and a Toorak shopping centre car park
is only good for reflections
made by sun on the glass
and the duco of four wheel drive's
and new Mercedes bends
until I'm squinting.

It's a delusion of false sophistication.
There are no romantic rivers and no artists
here.
The birds are sparrow scavengers with cheek
enough to bounce across my table
to see if I have left crumbs.
Mine are merely smoking butts and
the birds should know
that the habit isn't good for health,
but they move away
only if I make a motion of dismissal.

They'll be back.
it's the nature of addiction
to a quasi-cosmoplitan life,
and a delusion that I share,
in a Toorak car park cafe
over long, dark coffee.

December 2000

resigning from australia

are there no flowers in Australia?

well that cow Hansen was a passing thing
just a racist blip in a multicultural landscape
really nothing to worry about
and we all knew sense would prevail

not saying 'sorry' to the aborigines
was hard to take
but you know where these buggers
are coming from
they're frightened some poor part-black prick
with a left-wing lawyer on government money
will use an apology to squeeze compensation out of the
rest of us
it doesn't feel right but you can
sort of
follow the logic

and the children overboard thing was . . .

well look
there was an election to be won
and they knew damn well
they were on a winner
half the bloody country
is frightened to death of strangers
that are capable enough
to steer across thousands of miles
of nasty ocean in leaky boats
god knows what they could do
if we let them run loose
and now we can all be absolutely certain
that we elected a mob of sneaky
lying
shonks
to rule the country

Places and Locations

I'd hate to have to die wondering

yeh, yeh
anyone can make
a little currency-trading error
that costs the tax payers five or six
billion dollars
at least they didn't have to give it
to the aborigines

it's no secret what a turn-on
and what a come-on
fourteen-year-old girls can be
for some grown men
so
the governor-general not acting
on a church sex case -
back when he used to be a bishop -
and suggesting
it could have been the girls' fault
and not the vicars'
is pretty understandable I suppose
for a man of his generation
and clerical background

going bare knuckles over the fitness
of a high court judge
to preside over cases about the abuse of kids
based on the judges homosexuality
and a badly faked car log-book
is par for the course
for the rabid parliamentarian
running a vendetta against the judge for years
so that's no big deal

in any case
he wasn't *actively* encouraged
to abuse parliamentary privilege

of course he wasn't

and as usual the prime-bloody-minister
knew nothing about it at all so *he*
is not to blame
and it's really *nothing*
to do with the government

but the flowers have done it

having to listen to a captain of the Sally's
on radio
telling how a little girl has been in this country
for months -
all the time behind that bastard razor wire -
in some government-funded prison camp
for asylum seekers
that they've parked in the naked
forty-five-degree desert
with only one small tree in the compound
that a dog can piss up against
and her asking if this country
has any flowers in it . . .

that's too much

the guy from the Salvo's t
old how they held an appeal
and he went there with some bunches
stacked into his car
just pretty normal arrangements
from local florist shops
with a few native blooms thrown in

multiple buds wherever they could
so that as many kids as possible
could have one flower each . . .

well the poor mongrel says he only lasted
a half hour
before he had to leave
so he could have a cry
he was that overwhelmed
by the appalling gratitude
and the lingering hope

Places and Locations

and the deadness
in some of the eyes

shit

I nearly howled myself
just from listening to him

there's people there locked up
for over eighteen months
there's people there throwing themselves
onto the razor wire
there's people there on hunger strike
there's people there sewing their lips together
there's people there
thought they were escaping tyranny
there's people there that know an Australia
that I've never seen
and there's children there
don't even know
if we've got flowers

we call this *the lucky country*

lucky be buggered

the kids got some flowers

churches and others
gave them some flowers all right
but
I've had enough

I'm resigning from Australia
until some bastard in government
can give me a reason
to stop feeling ashamed

I quit

March 2002

school soiree - act 1

the flutes will be close to adequate
I have heard them in practice ad nauseum
and while wind rarely achieves greatness
there is hope that accompaniment
may minimise any untoward sounds

strings generally work well enough
with the violins often quite proximal
thanks to the efforts of Mister Suzuki
and I find it hard to believe
that the deep tones of cello or double bass
can be easily disturbed

there is always a budding virtuoso on piano
to relieve tension and to *ooh-ahh* over
perhaps scholarship alleviation of fees
has some small role to play in this

if we are fast and orderly however
there may just be time
to whip around the audience
with a sharply worded petition
before the start of the guitar ensem . . .

too late
act one has been called
we can only sit tight
in these student desks
smile and clap

school soiree - act 2

this is unexpected
the guitars seem to be playing as one

tonight there have been stumbles
in woodwind and flute
piano and violin
and the cello developed a stutter
but against expectations
the guitars have emerged from the pack

over the year we have watched
the acoustics *strum strum strum*
the electrics overload and overloud
the solos riff eccentric
sound notes but no heart

tonight the Chinese boy on lead
is moving his head
and I heard him say *two three four*
as they started to *twist and shout* that
you've really got me

the audience is of just the right age
there is spontaneous singing accompaniment
and the guitars have cracked the first smile
I have seen from them

> *well shake it up baby now*
> *you really got me*

school soiree - act 3

the violin with the round glasses
has already played
he sat oblivious through preceding acts
studying his own notes intently
then performing a gavotte impressively

now he is at rest
seated on the steps that rise tier by tier
to the top row
one of a gaggle of boys
who have already performed

the last act is also a gavotte
a difficult tune that has stumbled
and restarted once
already
all eyes are fixed
on the young performer creating dance
on centre stage

the gavotte-ist on the steps beside me
is transfixed
resting his own instrument against a leg
and holding with one hand
as his slender fingers
pick over the fingerboard
to play each note soundlessly
following and anticipating
every move made on stage

he would play again
if they asked

September 2002

signal for a sighting

when we stood towards the east
in mid morning
there was sun
bright against the hanging darkness
of heavy cloud
no longer either thunder or rain
though not long before
there had been both

from this vantage the angled planes of light
descended as veiled gold to cover
a greenness in the hills
that is unusual at this time of year
when the sun of summer
has generally baked the colour
from the undergrowth and leached the land
to a hungry nakedness
shaded in the hues and tones
of yellow-white and russet

turning we looked into the drifting black banks
of the storm now passed
the reflection of sun off cloud
giving the grass a luminosity in the aftermath
and the glow a signal to raise eyes
towards the massed shapes above
for a sighting of the rainbow

January 2002

study of a canberra fountain

at first glance it seems a Christmas tree
rising from a short trunk
widening then climbing to apex and point
water cascading down the circular sides

it is in fact a diamond inverted
triangular metal bars ascending to points
level upon level
a splay pattern of hexagonal facets

water streams from the cap of the upper level
down the metal tubes to a gutter
channels to the next cap
down metal tubes to gutter
through three levels
then slides facet to air

forming breaking and re-forming
unsupported triangles
that start wide then narrow to a thin stream
that strikes the surrounding pool
with its stray handful of well-wished coins
lapping gently past the reaching hand of a small child
draped across the brickwork barrier
before rising again through the trunk toward the apex
peak

the mother has risen now
time to journey on
within the movement of transient shoppers
in a misted background
that forms sub-text to the constant
of cascading water
in the endless cycle of a fountain
in the square
of the Canberra centre

September 2002

Places and Locations

the limitations of weather forecasting

they said to expect storms and thunder
heavy rains and large hail
away in the central district
not here

they gave no indication
that here in my own district
I would feel it coming
heat-trapped and oppressive
the air a little harder to breathe
stray droplets so large they hurt
when they strike and splatter

I was not told that the cumulo-nimbus
would be torn to hemorrhage light
blurred at the rent edges of cloud
to bleed a shade of grey all the way to ground

there was no clue given that the sky
would build white mountain ranges
or that I should allow sufficient time
to watch with craned neck and awe

there are serious limitations
to current weather forecasting capacities

I may write a letter

February 2002

the ms society sparrow

the MS Society sparrow has nested.
Squeezed between the white-on-blue
of a parking sign and tight-fit eaves.

More tunnel than nest, a single
chick demands from mother bird
more and more of the crumbs
and small donations she is offered at the cafe
in the immediate precinct
of the self-help charity.

The chick is fit to fly. Well, almost.
Flutter-wings and yellow-rim mouth,
wide open for the thrust of food
when mum is around. A harassed working girl
more likely from an inner suburb
where slums once lay and hard-doers
were much more common.

When mama-servant has gone, the chick
sits quiet in the aftermath of near disaster,
when his fluttering nearly threw him down.
Saved from a leaving-home moment
by tangling the nest around a leg, an anchor
to haul him in, restrain freedom
and avoid the need to learn to fly real fast.

Even in the affluence of Toorak, a girl
needs to keep her wits and strong suspicions.
She's seen me here, a stranger in her street,
watching, quiet, far too close for comfort.
Maybe it was a plume of blue-smoke
gave me away as it rose. Now
she won't come home, not until I'm gone.

Perhaps she isn't ready yet for visitors.
Could be the cleaning isn't done.

Places and Locations

The willingness of Master Chick to grab
the food he dropped with relish,
without mother,
and the self-satisfaction that he takes
from fast beak-scraping on the floor are a sign
that a clean-up might come soon.

Visitors may find a warmer welcome
when the young cock takes a step too far
and is gone to join the life down on
the streets. Won't be long he'll get to play
among the fat cats of Toorak streets.

February 2001

the pretty valley

there is too much green here
too many shades and depths
of vibrant grasses shrubs and trees
hills rolling into the distance
beautiful enough from some angles
to raise a lump in the throat but misplaced
on top of seams of rich brown coal

before the shape of the road crests
to reveal the valley
streaking pointer-lines
of ochre-shaded mist rise
in a slow drift action
to fill one small portion of heaven
then thin to wisps of nothing
brown of smoke contrasted against
the grey of cloud

this is the valley of Loy Yang A and B
of Hazelton and Yallourn
the valley of the power towns
Morwell   Moe   Traralgon   Wonthaggi
home to giant garish-yellow Ferris Wheels
with teeth that eat the land
spitting it in clods
onto conveyors
to fling light through darkness at a turning
of switches

in the day the four paired smokestacks
of Loy Yang
are an ocean liner steaming towards port
a line of twining smoke
trailed jaunty in the wind
but at night Yallourn shows visible
staring from left of the highway
with an unblinking red eye
a nagging discomfort
that keeps pace in the distance

perhaps harsher visions of this place
reveal a greater truth
than the elaborate greens of river flats
and undulating hills
for the towns are grown poor
and threadbare in their fabric
so long a repository for cheap housing
in the absence of employment
a final destination
for single mothers from the city
in search of modest rental

it is twenty years now into the restructuring
and though the property-men swear
it is still possible to live well here
you must not depend
on the richness of the brown coal
set below the verdant shadings
of an over-pretty valley
no
you cannot depend on the bastard coal
that has driven so many
who once loved this place
to leave

January 2002

there's codfish at yarrawonga

the Murray river's running higher
than it has in any time that I can easily recall
but when I was small
I never used to take notice
I only wanted fish to come onto my line
and let me be a kind of hunter

the river has been poorly for so long
she is like an old aunt with a disease
who's forgotten how to care for herself
and only hints at remembered glories
that reappear in a fleeting splendor
from time to time
to make us feel sadness for her

water surrounds the ghosts of long dead trees
where last summer I walked
on ancient forest paths
over dried and cracking mud
that made me feel withered
and old and responsible
for not caring hard enough
but now there is water again
and I am glad I cannot walk that way
anymore

a man in the pub said there's codfish
at Yarrawonga
said that somebody he knew
was catching them
maybe not as big as in the old days
but someone knows they're out there
and somebody is catching them
and maybe there's a little kid
that might get to be a hunter
and perhaps my aunt
will dress up in her splendor once again
if it rains

Places and Locations

if it only rains enough
for a mighty Murray

July 2000

Frank Prem

under the red dust

(from the home-offices of Clancy and Associates Pty Ltd)

I'd wanted to speak to him
and asked could he call me
it was a matter of detail
that needed his attention
and some thought

in the long days intervening
while waiting to hear from him
I have wondered
on occasion
whereabouts he may be now

the last time I heard of him
he was passing through Longreach
in a four-wheel-drive convoy
reaching out towards the Gulf
through country so dry
the red-dust is a coating
that settles on you through the day
like a layer of skin

and in the night-time I know well
there'll be a campfire and chilled beer
a little loud talk about the day and the drive
before the guitars come out
for strumming and singing
from his old tat-and-torn songbook
two thousand miles north
beneath the black and the stars

I am working
in a timber-lined brown room
that acts as makeshift office

Places and Locations

the windows are covered
to keep down the glare on the screen
while I doctor my way
through a report
pre-circulation
and pause
for another short moment
to wonder where he might be . . .

up beyond Longreach
well out of the range
of a mobile or land-line
underneath the red-dust
where his spirit is at home

June 2002

visitors

he doesn't overly care for visitors
is awkward in the hosting role
doesn't know where to put people
what to serve them or when
how to ensure they feel welcome
and are catered for

it is a long standing problem
a sense of inadequacy
that goes back as far in his life
as memory will take him

even when among those who are as close
as the feeling
of skin rubbed between two fingertips
he is overwhelmed by his own irrationality
regarding standards and decorum

when he visits others
he expects little
a seat placed out of harm's way
some conversation
and to be tolerated

a shivering stray
periodically embraced and warmed
then released intact

if at a gathering
he gradually becomes translucent
engages in slips of conversation
but attends the corners -
the outskirts of the crowd -
alone and uncomfortable
tenuous
half-dazed until he can escape
be alone for a moment
draw a deep breath
ease the tautness

Places and Locations

he likes people
observes them closely
drinks them in
and knows the urge to be of them
but finds no assurance
mistrusts linkages
leans towards the safety of a solitaire

and tends to not encourage visitors

~

it is quiet here today
the place next door is vacant
neighbours are at work
the traffic is nowhere near

sometimes when it's like this
I can almost imagine the sound
of a ray of sunshine
falling to earth
a warm sound
felt rather than heard

the house is freshly clean
everything newly in its place
I've noticed that tidiness exudes silence
eased only with the misplacement of objects
and return to a semblance
of interactive residence

I don't cope well with tidiness

the washing went on the line early
although already over a day old
memory for tasks is elusive
and one day can seem very like another

the mail is in
and I have circled the yard
front and back
to assess the progress of grass in the lawn
weed in the garden beds

lunch has been taken

it's so quiet
only my thoughts are loud
and my heartbeat

I could wish
almost wish

somebody might drop by

April 2003

Portrait Gallery

a man called merry christmas

a man called Merry Christmas
lives behind the Safeway,
among the boxes and bins
of this season of festive cheer.

He is a long white beard
and rat-nest shock of hair,
not combed since gone forever.

Blue eyes sparkling
under a new December sun,
above a toothless smile,
inside a wide and empty grin.

A booming, bellowed laugh

    (Ha-Ha-Ha)

cheers the sockless car park
from where he's sitting,
with his legs crossed,
by the Salvo's collection bin.

Mr Merry Christmas is a loner,
talk and laughing to himself.
No room for company
or strangers.
Forage isn't meant to share,
it is a solitary gift
subject to spoiling
if not eaten in the present,
after wrappings
of lettuce leaves and plastic paper
are sniffed once and discarded,
with an echo shout of triumph

    (Ha-Ha-Ha)

or the low dismay
of wiping hands on baggy jeans,
or on red and green
frayed braces.

He's happy Mr Merry Christmas

    (Ha-Ha-Ha)

from behind the Safeway store,
among the boxes and the bins
of another festive season

    (Ha-Ha-Ha)

December 2000

acting on one leg

a friend of mine is a one-legged man
who once was an over-weight thespian
fell on the stage in rehearsal
broke an ankle
picked up infection in the hospital
lost his leg

he is a jolly man
who runs to two new prosthesis every year
removes the current choice from time to time
in sock and shoe
to stand alone on his work-desk
painted in the stripes
of his football team colours

occasionally he throws it at someone
to catch them unawares

sometimes I feel
that I have missed the catch

I am off-balance and destabilised
like a one-legged actor
whose *exit stage-left*
is a fall
amid a tangle of forgotten lines
and missteps

2002

after his 'women'

but what do you make of women like that
they kept coming
they were young and seemed to know
what they wanted
at least for a little while

and he was older and ugly
writing about his philandering ways
the practice of faithless love

sometimes it seems the more you confess
the more sin you get to keep

even when he knew that he was bad
he kept on going
even when they knew that he was bad
they kept coming
la la
la
la

bukowski
it's really good to meet you
I've been hearing about you now
for years

I think I like the way you
mark your paper
like the way you hold your alcohol
the way you just keep travelling

serendipity
out on the streets

and if you're lonely
if you're working
or sleeping
if you're wondering what the hell to do . . .

she's on the telephone

she's in your doorway

she's yelling things
from the middle of the road
screaming out she loves you
really hates you
really wants you in her bed

she wants to own the words you say
wants them written in a one-to-one
that's hers to keep
but . . .

they're already out there
they're flying through the air
if I put my hand up now
I'll catch them
halfway right around the world

twenty years later

oh well

are they still chasing you
charlie b
wherever in hell
you are

keep your head down
your paper straight
and keep on pinning them
right onto the page

April 2003

all anyone can ask

well I don't think he's much better
than my benny really
in fact
in some ways he's worse off because
benny gets a disability support pension
and that at least means something
to people
about the fact that ben can and can't
do some things
as well as other people can
whereas he -
on the other hand -
doesn't look
like he has anything wrong with him
so people expect him to be able to work
and think and plan
in a normal way and I'm telling you
I don't think he can do it

rubbish
he's a born fool who can't stick at anything
and goes running home
whenever things go wrong for him
I've got no time for him
why can't he just stick with a job
why does he have to throw it in straight away
and then make excuses for himself
he's a lazy no-hoper
and nothing but trouble
your benny is different
he was sick and it did something to his brain
we know ben mostly looks ok but really isn't
it's a different situation

I think that really
he's a little simple
I don't mean that he's stupid
because I'm actually pretty sure
that he's reasonably bright
but
he seems simple to me
in the way that a dreamer is simple
I think he lives on a different plane somehow
where whatever happens inside his head
is more real than what is going on around him
I don't think he can cope
with the demands out here
it's very sad really because no-one can see it
and they're very intolerant of him

I don't think he'll ever quite manage
on his own
will always need a little bit of help
a lot like benny

he's going to drain his mother and father
is what he's going to do
they've done so much for him already
and splat
there he is a burden on them again
it's just selfishness
pure and simple
I don't think they'll ever get him
off their hands
at least your benny does his best
and that's all anyone can ask

yes
that's all anyone can ask

April 2003

an accustomed gaze

he is standing at the window
staring hard across Beach Road
past the yellow buoy
that marks the channel
away into the distance
of Geelong

the restaurant is a rattle around him
but he has left his party
the gun-metal blue
of the water
as the sun goes down
has caught his eye
drawn him to this sight
of the bay at evening

it is obvious at a glance
he needs to be there
one with the rocking waters
tension shows
in the clench of jaw
and forward leaning posture
tuned
to near-flight

only for a moment
then gone
replaced by a sigh
a softer gaze
and a brief contact
of fingertips to glass
before return to a place
at table
re-engagement
through light conversation

there is no comment passed
they are accustomed
to his ways

March 2003

assertive gestures

she is standing in the half-light
of early morning
an intent gaze
fixed through the glass sliding door
beyond the green sparseness
of occasional pinus
across an acreage of sand
that's almost glowing in this light
and to the water

she is repeating gestures
a beckoning come-hither motion
of the hand and a finger
concentrating hard on the point
where a line of rising blue
is first apparent

the point at which brilliant white
gleams for a brief moment
recedes
then rises again
stronger
in a solid line of agitation and froth
surging to fall over itself
stressed green
intermingled with the blue and the white

she is gesturing to draw the waves
to summon the foam
ordering an alignment of swell and breaker and wash

it is a difficult job
sometimes it can take all day

July 2002

at doyle's

she wandered through the tables
like a waitress, there at Doyle's.
From the menu,
taste of rhythm in her form.

And she swept the path before her
clear of rabble rousing noise.
In her eyes
flash lightning, like a storm.

From every man, a naked glance,
more furtive from the boys.
Fresh captives,
to an idea they just formed.

One was left, mouth open
at a side-step made with poise.
Interception foiled,
not close to warm.

Because...

She's not there.
She's in another place.
She's not there,
it's just a picture.

She's away somewhere,
gone beyond the limit.
She's away somewhere,
I think you missed her.

It's only in unguarded times
the strain of something shows.
Emptiness,
concealed inside a style.

If you look too closely,
she'll colour like a rose,
then gone.
You won't see her for awhile.

Portrait Gallery

She's safest when you're distant,
with nothing too disclosed.
Just watch her,
rewarded with a smile.

When she cries like a lover,
you're not supposed to know.
At Doyle's,
the drink of choice is guile.

Because...

She's not there.
It's only tiny fragments.
She's not there.
She's scattered pieces.

She's away somewhere.
Destination hidden.
She's away somewhere.
till need decreases.

Until then, she wanders, like a waitress,
through the tables, there at Doyle's . . .

October 1999

axeman blues

the axeman is a player
attacking the blues
with plastic picking aids
on the fingers of his right
a prosthesis on the smallest finger of his left
to make the black bottleneck come alive
bend and quiver
and beat

there's fifteen in the crowd
young and old
got their eyes closed and swaying
fifteen more so quiet
there's nothing between
audience and axeman

singing just a little but not too much
the axe is a voice on its own
and that's enough

I think that's enough

July 2001

baby's bedtime

baby doesn't read much anymore
in the evenings
her eyes become too tired from the page
and an accumulated feeling
like staring into light too long
makes her rub
to find more natural sensations

she was always baby to her brothers
and her late father
at fifty eight and climbing it's getting late
to start growing up now
when lines are etched into her features
and a rug has to keep winter knees
in circulation

baby takes a cup of tea with a half of honey
just on bedtime
it seems a fitting way to mark the passing
of awake time into the hours of sleep
before the ascending weariness
of a footstep at a time up the stairs
and to her room

the blanket is set on *high*
to guarantee warmth of bedding
it seems a little like a decadence
but
who alive will know
and the comfort of a warm bed
is like mother's touch recalled from long ago

in the darkness the upstairs room
is almost soundless
with nothing out of the ordinary to be heard
just the gentle rise of baby's breath
as she settles into a steady sleep
to carry her past one day and on
into the next

May 2000

curtain down (for jenny langley)

the performance is done
The curtain is down
The show, at last, is over.

Listening behind the stage
  (Hear the applause).

It's been a masterly play
Comedy! Passion! Romance!
How slow the passion expends itself ...

If you listen, even now
  (Hear the applause).

You have enacted so well
With your dance, with your song
(But) the chorus, at last, refrained.

If you listen - ever faintly -
  (Hear the applause),

The timing was right
The show ran like clockwork
But this time, at least, is over.

If you listen, O, careful now
  (Hear the applause).

We are all gathered here
Supporting cast and crew
(don't believe the show could be over),

We hope, if we're loud enough
  O Yes, we hope, that if we're loud enough
    You may hear our applause.

July 1998

don't ring before seven

my dad likes a drop to drink
he's loved it all his life
and my mother says
don't ring before seven o'clock
he won't be home and you know
he hates to miss saying hello
let him get home from the pub
before you call

my dad does business holding
a pot of ice cold beer
mum says he's spent enough
to own the entire bar
but that's where customers come
with an ask for a job to be done
and to seal it in the foam
of golden lager

my dad used to drink a bit
when he was young
mama told me all about it
how strong spirits would turn his head
on the kitchen wall you can almost
see the stain where a plate struck
when he was offered a burnt dinner
but she missed

my dad can surely hold his grog
mutti says he complains now
of discomfort in the stomach
but he'll drink a stubby after lunch
while working in the shed
and won't miss the happy hour
unless his body is especially low
feeling unwell

Frank Prem

I call my dad Sundays after seven
ma says hello and how am I
then he takes a turn on the phone
to tell me all about things

and if I get to visit for awhile
around five he'll catch my eye
it's time to go

May 2001

dancer

Featured in the Ozpoet Showcase July 1999 - Movement and Dance

Toe, toe
Spin
To left.

Run, run
Leap
Scissor
Leap
Scissor.

Point
Hold
Balance
Hold.

Lift, lift
Turn
To right.

Flow, flow
Flex
Kick
Flex
Kick.

Fold, fold
Split
To ground.

Rise, rise
Bow
To front
Bow
To front.

.
.
.

Only her shoes
A reminder.

August 1998

jen

Flower of the morning
Dewdrops of night
Thunderclap warning
Silhouette light
Earthly adorning
Feelings and sight.

July 1998

lollypop man

he's a jolly un-english man
owner of a thick handlebar moustache
and a smiling fat face
above a red stripe white coat
and a sign that says

    stop

weekdays he is at the primary school
with a wave as I go past and a melody of

    e-lo

every day he walks the children
to the centre of the crossing
then returns to kerb-side
and waves his greeting song
at the cars that pass

    e-lo

in a rumbling surprise of deep voice
that might have just arrived
from a coffee-land
but right now it belongs
to a wide fat smile
on the dark skinned face
of a jolly traffic stopper
at a place where children
walk across the road

the voice within a smile
at the crossing that belongs
to a Cheltenham jolly llypop man

    e-lo

2001

mietta o'donnell

mietta o'donnell died today
i never knew her
but i visited her house
dined on her cuisine
took pride in reading her
in the papers
i don't really know why
she just seemed to be there
a part of my town
and of its life

mietta o'donnell is gone today
this place is a little poorer
so i will buy a deep red wine
coloured blood against the light
and raise a glass
a rich red glass
to bid her well
upon her journey

January 2001

old trevallion

The only fans of old Trevallion
are shifting the air above his head,
as he drags a quiet metal note
from deep in the body
of a bruised guitar.

You need to listen closely
to eliminate the rhythm of blades
keeping a different time,
to a different song
that sounds a little too mechanical.

Only three or four in the early crowd
have come to see him.
He doesn't draw many, any more.
Perhaps he never did
but, he's played for a long time

in so many broken places,
with that quiet metal note above
the soft humming of a chorus
whirred to a beat
that feels a little too mechanical.

Some notes don't play
as sweetly as they used to.
Some days the old guitar won't play at all,
just chords that are nothing like
the melodies they ought to be
but,
a day without Trevallion plucking someplace
is the feeling of a hearts demise.

As long as there's a fan somewhere
he'll play those quiet metal notes,
even if they sound
a little bit
too mechanical.

2001

perpetually young

bumped into a girl
that went to school with my sister.
Eighteen to fifty is a fright
that can catch you unawares.
Look into her face,
see a portrait painted of her mother.
What happened to the girl?
She doesn't look the way
that she did.

My sister still looks much the same to me,
I've been growing older, too,
keeping up with her
and her face doesn't look too strange.
But the only face I remember for her friend
is a girl, never been about, never stepped around
in the world.

And now she looks as though
she could almost be someone's grandma.
How did that get to come about,
and why am I still so young?
I'm still very young.

Don't creep up on me,
behind my back, after so long.
You could scare me ancient, send me pictures,
keep me up to date,
I don't want to have to
feel quite that old.
Keep pace, we'll go down together
and we can both stay young.

We'll stay perpetually young,
again.

January 2001

Frank Prem

praying for grandfather

featured in Map of Austin Poetry (MAP) #186-1, June 2001

> *We will pray for grandfather, she said,*
> *in the hope that he will develop*
> *a sense of humour.*
> *And we will pray that he becomes less tired.*
>
> *He has been tired, you know,*
> *for all of his life.*

She smiled as she said it,
and reclaimed a stitch that had fallen,
rocking to the cadence of her own speech
and the clacking rhythm of the needles.

> *It is difficult to be the man*
> *of the household . . .*

She was speaking almost to herself,
as though in a reverie,
with the rest of us forgotten.

> *. . . so much burden and responsibility,*
> *for the earning of the money,*
> *the making of decisions*
> *and having to stay aloof*
> *to bear failures and mishaps.*
> *To stifle the questions that are unbecoming*
> *when directed to the man.*
> *We will pray grandfather recovers*
> *from his tiredness,*

she said,

Portrait Gallery

and pray that he does not need
to be so aloof
in order to avoid having to explain
the shortfall in the household accounts
which worsened last Saturday,
and
on quite a few Saturdays before

Why,
even I may recover
a sense of humour . . .

and with that her smile broadened
and there was a notable gleam in her eyes,
as though she'd said a wickedly delicious thing,
as she rocked and knitted.

April 2001

ronnie's other guy

published in 'Transparent Words 2', July 2000

ronnie loves davey but
she's got a habit
of kissing another guy

davey doesn't know
anything about it because
it only happens when
she's drifting
and her mind is painting pictures

she's with davey
right until her eyes close
but then
she's walking under a moon somewhere
holding hands with a guy
whose face isn't clear
and she's touching him

her feet are making ripples
in the water
when she stands
high up on her toes
and moves her lips to his
in a soft kiss
that isn't davey

ronnie loves davey
every minute of the day
she doesn't look at anybody else
but
in the darkness when he touches her
and her eyes go automatic closed
she has a little habit
of kissing another guy

May 2000

the osteo

on wyndham street
just melbourne-side of the railway line
tara the osteo smiles
at a customer come for a massage
and a cracking good time
she smiles

a large girl
who uses her weight
to lean right down on an out-breath
cracking a back
and making him laugh
while he lacks air

it's a laugh of surprise
and relief
but tara is sure in her handling
and understands manipulation

she says half of her skill
is psychology
making the customer talk
feel at home
while she tends
to aches caused by slouches
and age
and a lack of due care
through the passage of a lifetime

tara the osteopath
is smiling
almost saintly
while ringing the till
for twenty-five dollars
after insurance

wishes him well
to take care
and not neglect exercise
to come back in a fortnight
on the monday
and to walk straight
until then

2006

value for money

excuse me,
can you lend me two dollars?

hello sandy,
can you lend me two dollars please?
my name is john, sandy,
and i'm pleased to meet you, too

yes, sandy,
it IS a lovely day

i live locally, sandy,
and I walk around the street here
quite often
i have lived here
for a long time now, sandy

i want to buy some cigarettes
and something to drink
thank you, sandy
yes,
i hope to see you here again, too, sandy
goodbye, sandy

excuse me,
could you lend me two dollars?

September 2000

whose six-pack? whose scotch?

there are three of us in a babbling hotel,
close to the happy hour.
He is older than I,
younger than my father.
A man full of stories
about the town that he left
when he was young.

A rich balladeer,
unique in his capacity to reflect
through the escapists fortune
of having been away.

> In all the years till my father died,
> when I was a youth
> and when I was already a man,
> I never once supplied, or offered
> to supply, beer or whisky or wine.
>
> When I brought my mates around home,
> we drank his beer.
> When my brothers and I came to visit,
> we could not retire to our beds
> while there was a drop left
> in the whisky bottle
> that he always had available,
> even if it was just the two of us
> doing the drinking.
>
> You know, I never even thought
> of offering to supply it,
> whether drink or food.
> Of course, I realise
> that he would have been offended
> if I'd ever done such a thing, but,
> especially since he died,
> I've thought about it a lot
> and wished that . . .

sometimes

*I'd bought a six-pack, or a bottle of scotch,
and at least made the gesture.*

My own father responded,

*well, that's just the way things were
in those days, and now
you probably do the same
for your own kids.*

I looked at my father, and thought,

yes, that's the way you have always been.
Perhaps I should get a six-pack
or a slab of beer to offer you,
and see what you have to say to that.

Meanwhile,
drink up gentlemen, it's my shout.
What'll you have?

April 2003

My Neighbourhood

My Neighbourhood

a disparity of views

the parrots have enjoyed the rain
a whole flock of the ring-necked little buggers
flapping around preening and yapping
to each other
like christmas just came
the mynah is hunched and gloomy
and a wattlebird looks
for an empty branch

it's winter after all
and the silly fools
probably don't know any better

June 2001

Frank Prem

a fragment of clouds

i have been watching flights of cloud
overlapping layers of bulbous deep grey
that lighten
then proceed through shades of white
to painful brightness
as an upper strata is caught in the last reach
of the dying sun
while the collective cumulus below
casts moist grasping wisps
across a sky fragment
of bleak black temper
portending rain and storm
or smothering
by wet nimbus pillow
if the air slips lower

May 2001

a new cloud

I have found a new kind of cloud
a new presence in the atmosphere

it's a big bustling bruiser
covered in six-pack greys
and whites

shoulders its way through crowded spaces
like a bulked-up user of supplements
to raise mighty celestial weights
and ethereal masses

the gleaming big-boy smile
full of dazzle from the reflecting sun
is all confident
all powerful

introducing:
musculo-nimbus
wide-boy of the skies

August 2002

a private eye

naked on decking
the heat of middle day unravels layers
renders them unnecessary
in this seclusion

wearing a cigarette
I gaze into the double-storey
across the road
through the street-facing window
to the corner upright of a stairway
people
walk up
bounce down
engaged with domesticity
they do not know I exist
that I
watch

exposed
naked
open but unseen

I am
the fleet glimpse into other lives
the purveyor
it is I who am private

I

January 2003

a resemblance

in some ways that pigeon resembles me
a plump waddler easily startled

it pulls its head and stomach down
to a point just over and in front of its legs
before a launch into the air
accompanied by frantic flapping of wings
to ensure lift off

perhaps if I could centre my gravity
in just that way
I could launch into the same air

      coo

August 2001

Frank Prem

a sound of home

it is raining
a light intermittent patter
that I can hear
tottering across my roof

this house has cathedral ceilings
not so very high
but an A-frame none-the-less
there is no distance
between the wood-panel ceiling
that I see
and the red metal roof
that is amplifying raindrops
in a peaceful pattern
that has comforted
since childhood

I believe I may like it here

November 2002

a spring smoke ring

it is still cold here
surprising when the spring progression
so often throws up glorious days
of promising sun and glowing warmth

the evidence is presented by a wattlebird
ugly grey-speckled harridan of the garden
red-cheeked raucous and discordant squawker
of alleged birdsong
raising its head from among the leaves
of a flowering gum
to startle with its booming call
and blow a misty smoke ring
into the sky

October 2001

a summer

this guy is singing about the summer of '69

about his mateship with the gang
that he used to knock around with
he finishes each punch line with a
woah yeah

he's on a cd playing in the background
while three girls and a couple of boys
who weren't born
for a decade and a half after '69
are linking arms and swaying
singing the song out word for word
and I get an image - a flashback
to *my* summer

I can see ted and ian
johnny and noel
jenny denise judy and the rest
in the early hours of a darkened room
linked heads-together into a circle
so that nothing could break the chain
swaying back and forwards and in and out
shouting out at the darkness and to the night
that

> *nothing's going to change our world*
> *no nothing's going to change our world*

and then

> *baby says she's traveling*
> *on the one after nine-o-nine*
> *move over once*
> *move over twice*
> *come on baby don't be cold as ice*

My Neighbourhood

I see it all clearly

the kids in front of me are still linked
and moving in this
their summer of 2003

and I am in motion too

linked arm-in-arm with my gang
back in a summer that burned
a long time ago

December 2003

a surprise of iris

this garden holds surprises
today it is the reaching gold
and yellow butter shades of iris
speckled brown at the heart
showing signs that the day
has been a harshness
beneath the relentless beat
of summer sun

they have emerged from
the anonymous green of nowhere
these brave few flowering shoots
past the peak of their season
but arriving timely
to lift my spirits lest they too
wilt under the judgemental glare
of the merciless orb above

just a moment no more
and then the gushing cool of water
rehydration to return firmness and stoicism
to plant and bloom and spirit
for tomorrow may bring more
and we do well to be ready
for surprises

January 2003

black cloud low

black cloud
low sky
aeroplane towards me
gulls away in "U" formation
break apart
re-form

last sun
searching beams
pinpoint radiant light
on dazzle reflections
one towards me
fifty-three away

June 2001

an aspendale chorus

      reep-reep-reep-reep-reep
      cree-cree-cree-cree-cree-cree

the night is silent
no movement in the streets
low cloud seems to enclose
to hug the houses quiet

beyond the development
is a surrounding wetland
green brush stands high along the roadsides
holding its secrets to itself
there are birds
but they are only visible
when flying above
pelicans and hawks
ducks sometimes

it is so still this night
the hum murmur of distant traffic
on the through-road
serves only to background
a multi-toned chorus
performed ensemble
by the Aspendale frogs

      reep-reep-reep-reep-reep
      cree-cree-cree-cree-cree-cree

November 2002

My Neighbourhood

an avian reminder of cold

a pretty scene
the upper corner of the window is aglow
sunshine is radiated off pointillised
wattle blossom

it is the movement of a bird
that has caught my eye
drawn attention to the scene
as it flits between wattle-yellow
and the faded red of a persistent grevillea
there is a stark contrast
between this illusion of bright warmth
and the hanging chill of my office
where an impression of cold
seems ever present
in the dulled staccato movement
of my hands jerking across the keyboard

in my feet

through my knees

surrounding my buttocks

everywhere beneath my work-clothes

stupid bird
those curtains should not be left open

August 2002

another familiar layer

the window is a water fall
drops winding on their way
in a journey that veers and sways
ever downwards

vision is less than clear
impeded by a grey-white pall
of mist that holds on to conceal
the weather

hiding in a cosy room
heater set to high
encounters with familiar things
give comfort
no challenge in the same old plans
reworked for one more day
no danger in the warm
of repetition

think it must be raining now
the sound is beating down
nothing much that i can do
to stop it

draw the blind to shut away
exposure to another burst of cold
and don the coat familiar
and another layer

May 2000

april fools day flyers

idiosyncratic red and white and grey flyers
they hint at disaster just ahead
accidental chaos behind

the magpie is black and white directness
the cockatoo is sulphur crow-raising raucousness
but steady and straight nonetheless

but these clowns fly multi-level bobbing paths
like a car
with its wheels attached off-centre
and poor front end alignment
that drags them
resistant
first to the left
then the right

they are well named fools t
hese galahs

April 2002

awaiting a call to arms

the dust motes are aggressive today
massing
they have used the slight swirl
of a still-cool breeze
to hurl themselves against my legs
this could be what I have anticipated
an opening assault
the only real question
whether they can organise

sustain

the signs have been ominous for some time

grey streaks on clothing
retrieved from the floor

secret tracking of footprints
only apparent in certain light
and a sure sign my movements are followed

stray rays of sunlight a revelation
of the extent
of opposition numbers

truly it appears I am surrounded
while the plotting proceeds apace
through furtive gatherings
clustered in the corners of each room
spread along the breadth
of baseboards

they have allies
the cobwebs too have been active

rappel lines descend from the ceiling
in a stealthy approach
progressed incrementally
at a pace
that has the stamp of inevitability about it

My Neighbourhood

but I have been waiting
for forces to be unleashed

I am aware of their gambits
and have planned exit and escape
to a nicety

the attack this day is a sign
if my plans should be astray
the requirements may be drastic

but back-up
is available if required
good plans always incorporate
a second level of response

concealed within a hallway cupboard
unopened and unobserved since the haste of my arrival

the *Indoor Broom* awaits my call to arms
and if the worst comes to the worst
I will sweep the floor with them

October 2002

blossom possum

there's a possum - a ringtail -
waltzing on a wire.

More like a determined waddle,
to speak the truth.
It's not long gone dark and the little guy
is on a mission between the poles,

he jumps from one line to another
at the conjunction,
turns a right angle to cross
over the road and above my head,
without a pause.

It must be too early to be curious
when there's a branch that's full of blossom
just a short way up ahead.

And then he's gone.

September 2001

blur day

eight thirty o'clock on post office corner
fifteen minutes to park
ought to be enough for me
i only want papers
and mail

bills to pay
but they can wait until
my head's caught up to me
i can't think straight
this early

the alley is all supermarket vans
and supplies
for the bustle of another pension pay
feels like already this day's a blur
and i haven't started yet

maybe i should crawl back into bed

September 2001

born to dance

cheltenham is near winter
the air deep-chilled
on these still mornings
when cold settles
to make breath smoke and drift
lazy in the early silence

it is quiet here
the street is sleeping
and I am alone
to see the broad-leaf dancer
on the green carpet of nature strip
beneath a lifeless tree
across the road

rising tall
four straight shoots stand
unmoving and rigid
surrounding a colleague
with an unstoppable
need to move
in the urgent vibrations
of a private rhythm

some of us are born to dance
even if we have to dance alone
in the chill silence
of a Cheltenham morning

May 2001

My Neighbourhood

busy day clouds

sometimes even in a busy day
the sky demands attention

yesterday was patterned white
streaky lines and commas
a shoal of driven jellyfish
swimming eastwards on the current
of a constant wind
blowing somewhere high above me

today is lightly covered wall to wall
with cumulus sub-stratum
blackened blobs of damp intent
bleeding one into another
like a watercolour blend on a page
stretched across forever

stretched
wide enough to fill the hours
of this busy day

I don't remember anymore
what I was doing

November 2001

call for an inquiry

this morning while the air was still
and the cold imposed a silence
over the outer suburbs I was caught
by a shock of surprise
when I glanced away from the road
to see the green familiarity of paddocks
with stray trees and occasional cows
stretching to meet the shape of distant hills
faint through the white smoke
of a rising mist

like the countryside of my childhood

is this small piece of yesterday unworthy
of conversion into dwelling or street or park?
where are the developers
and
should there not be
some kind of inquiry?

June 2000

chick magnet

sometimes they just won't leave him alone

he has commandeered a table by himself
coffee　　　　a novel half an hour
of peace
but she has come uninvited
ignoring other available options
to sit at his table
very close
an intruder into private space

he is now concentrating hard on the novel
working at ignoring her
but it is difficult
every inward breath
is an aural extravaganza
every exhalation is accompanied
by a sterterous moan
soft but audible

she leans towards him and she is a talker
a fidget
forever moving in the corner of his vision

she speaks something at him
he doesn't respond
beyond gripping the book tighter
a serviette is manhandled into shape
the sound of her nose being blown -
like a fanfare of trumpets
at the gates of heaven -
is startlingly loud

he jumps

and breathy moaning is now accompanied
by the vigorous snorts and snuffles
of a moist process of adjustment

THAT MUST BE A GOOD BOOK

he has to look at her
a large-breasted cardiganned septuagenarian
all gappy smile and innocent curiosity

yes it's a good book

there are some days
when you couldn't beat them off
if you had a large stick

October 2002

My Neighbourhood

company for a magpie

a magpie and a wagtail
are keeping odd company on the park
the magpie has no partner and is not part
of a gang of bachelors
he bustles on the ground
in a few running steps this way and that
pauses to assess
and then hurries forward again
the wagtail matches the running movements in a manner
almost mocking
but whereas the magpie is all chest and legs
the wagtail is a tail-ticker who insinuates
an occasional curlicue of flight

I wonder what the magpie has done
to achieve ex-communication
it would be more usual to find his kind
living as part of a thuggish band
of delinquent warblers
marauding over claimed territory
I wonder too about his association
with the scallywag-tail
the grim beaker and the clown

I suppose even a solitary misfit
is entitled to a mate

September 2002

coriander

green groceries in safeway has a sign
that says

    coriander

but it's a bit mixed up
and I don't know what coriander looks like
but the lady shopping here beside me
must know and
I ask her . . .

she hasn't got a clue

so I ask the young man
steadily putting packets onto shelves
he says

    is that a vegetable?

and
his mate doesn't know
so what am I to do

I'll ask the grandmother
who's just wandered up beside the cucumbers

    excuse me . . .

    no

she says

    it might be this one
    but you know
    people my age use the dried stuff
    I can't help you sir . . .

My Neighbourhood

    is it
    this bunch here with the delicate root . . .

well
even if it is it's such a saggy thing
I was told it had to be fresh . . .

the fruit and veg consultant out the back
sends news
wrapped in green and plastic
with the message to

    take these home
    and you can fake it
    sir

well
I *hope* I have a bunch of coriander

oh
and onions

October 2001

crushed flowers

someone's been in
the garden
with hardened feet

instead of
sipping fragrance
there's a carnage behind
each clumsy footstep

there are marks of destruction
to structures hand-grown
inside a gentle design
of beauty and order
through time

there was no malice
just a judgmental
misplacement
of one step
at a time

and at the turning
it seems that
nothing is left
but a lost
lingering perfume

from the bruises
of tangential petals
lining a ruined array
in the wreckage
from a crushing
of flowers

March 2000

My Neighbourhood

dead shrub

the shrub is dead
there is no doubt of that
a collection of fragile
and empty dry branches
suspended pointlessly

until an angle of falling light
reveals twenty-two intricate webs
woven in identical silk
patterning varied only as much as needed
to capture and embrace those twigs
in immediate vicinity

and two small dragon flies
clinging precariously
against a brisk breeze
reflecting gloriously
the sun

April 2001

ghosts

there are three ghosts
side by side apparitions
on the bricks of the wall
outside the house

large bulbous white shapes
with darkened eyes
reminiscent of a faded memory
of comic books

a change of angle shows them
as patches of light
filtered through the willow tree
but till then
I thought they might speak

September 2001

My Neighbourhood

going coo-coo

featured in the e-zine Caught in the Net 2 May 2001

There are pigeons on my rooflines.
The sun is still low and highlights
a bump where each fat, grey
ball of feathers is coo-cooing away
as though its life depends on it.
Maybe it does.

The sun is a threat today.
Still hot from the day just gone
and full of menacing promise
of a sweltering meltdown to come.
I will sauna in my workplace.
There is no relief beyond
the feverish recycling of heated air,
the best my pedestal fan can do.

And work is both bane and salvation
for this day, with no place to run
from the heat and nowhere to hide
from tasks accumulated. The hope
is of becoming lost in the intricacies
of policy and procedure, submission
and correction, and change,
for its own sake.

The coo-cooing pigeons have moved off.
It is time to start, to seek a cooler place
in my mind and lose myself there.
As though my life depends on it.
And, maybe, it does.

February 2001

Frank Prem

grinning in shadow

the line marking the beginning of car
and the end of sunshine
is stark in the glare of emergence
from indoors
nothing is visible in the deep shadow
except a rictus grin of teeth and tongue

black cat is sleeping

a mouth breather it seems

November 2001

gunshot

i think it was a gunshot
what did you think
it might have been?
could have been the rattle-bang
sound of a tired car
could have been anything
but maybe it was gunshot
somebody taking on the street
they used to do that
in the old wild west
chelsea's about as close to that
as i have ever seen
somebody dial emergency
get some help out to check it out
maybe we need police
to answer fire with fire
in case it was a gunshot
i swear it sounded that way
don't you think it might have been?
i'm not inclined to imaginings
i know i heard the sound
single shot on a quiet night
a problem solved
and nobody any wiser
i think it was the sound of a gun
and i'm going to read it
the morning papers

August 2000

harbinger

the movement caught my eye
a sudden motion repeated
like a nervous twitch

the clouds are a pure white against blue
high up and distant this bright morning
and in the flowering cherry
a small fantail is ticking its tail

neither a wagtail nor a scissors-grinder
unless quite young
but a new bird among the blossom
yet another sign of spring

I will name the bird harbinger

September 2001

hypothesis

the mice seem to have woken

the white is purposeful and fast
carrying wood shavings
from one end of the cage to the other
filling in the base of the wheel
the brown is attentive   supervising

there seems no likelihood of cessation
perhaps they intend to fill the wheel entire
no more going round in circles

perhaps it is nesting behaviour
although I believe
there is only one gender between them

more likely it is proof positive
of my small experimental hypothesis

pizza crust causes hyperactivity

November 2001

less than average rain

published in The Lakes and Longbeach Gazette, May 2000 edition.

walk along the backroads
of summer
hot wind touching your face
the shimmers prancing capers
are silvery devils in the heat of the day

there's no respite from the brown
of a baking land

hold out your arms
for water
no sign of rain no cloud
long trails of white to sydney
fade to blue in an empty sky

with no fall of sweet salvation
from above

there's nothing too surprising
in the dry of the dust and dirt
the illusions still dancing
come from the springtime

the aching thirst of too much sun
brings an end to last hollow hopes
and the truth about the season
is arriving home

again

January 2000

magpie submission

there was a magpie yesterday
rolled over on his back
feet in the air like submission
while another gave a threatening glance
and acted as though it might take a feather
to demonstrate command

I saw it happen again today
one in a crowd of five rolled over
exposed its place in the pecking order
at the bottom   on its back
then leapt up as if to show
it didn't really happen
like it didn't signify a thing

next year there'll be a new bachelor
young and fresh into the gang
next year there'll come a time
to show stature in the flock
sneak a little feather peck
and watch another fellow on his back

September 2001

minor adaptation

mynah birds are clever little critters
survivors able to adapt
to inner city and suburban conditions
I heard they are good mimics
within the urban situation
often startling in renditions
of other birds and city sounds
but they know their limits
and won't be drawn to the point
of adaptive foolishness
mistrustful of excessive assimilation

though seeming aware of the rules
the yellow beaked babbler sped
from jaunty walk   to ungainly run
finally flying from the centre point
rightly assuming that right of way
for a mynah on a zebra crossing
may not yet be recognised by all

2001

My Neighbourhood

mysterious woman (and duck)

she's a bit of a mystery woman
lives two doors up
behind a high brick wall
that's a little out of the usual
on our avenue

an ageing blonde with slavic black brows
and a painful limp

speaks italian

friendly enough to me
and to the lesbian girls next door
and to old frank over the road
but keeps herself to herself
behind that high fence
attractive in a reserved
'don't get too close' kind of way

none of which explains
the flash of brown
with teal at the outstretched tips
that announced itself
with a kind of braying honk
seconds before I saw it pass
sideways on and at a rate of knots
along the piece of road
visible from my driveway

I can tell you that it landed
and I saw it give a shake
that started at beak and ended
in an ecstasy of waggled tail
before it sauntered under the gateway
and disappeared into the womans' yard

she's a mysterious woman that mira

but curiously attractive

September 2001

pink snow

the yard is covered in pink-white snow
the same colour as tonights sunset
the white ornamental cherry
is losing its flowers
and our lawn is pink in snow

October 2001

My Neighbourhood

picture window

the oversized glass is noticeable
eye-catching in its own right
taller than a man standing
almost as wide as the room
boundaries marked by the thick
full-height timber of adjoining sashes
one each side of the main window

the outlook presents in squared format
as through the view-finder of my instamatic

this morning the sun
only part-emerged
from behind remnants of rain and cloud
has added a lustre to the green grasses
of the eastern aspect
a serene expanse in the centre
of this postcode Malvern
the heart of suburbia
bordered by highway and shopping town
franchise fast-food and higher education
as far from the lapping waters of my Bay
as I am able to imagine
and yet a small compensation

in the foreground
advantaged by morning light from above
and parkland beyond
the slender she-oak
a stoop of dangled soft-needle leaves
colored wet and dark against the peeping sun
holds a tremble of diamond at each tip

a bright one hundred
that glisten like light
played over a treasure chest
framed in the living-picture window
of number thirty-eight

2002

preparations (two in the kitchen)

there's two in the kitchen
and no room to swing
the cat has to be told to leave
while the raw meat is waiting
for a cut down to size
and a marinade to soak it
as only three of four burners have
life left to raise pressure and boil
pontiac potatoes right over the sides
of their pots with a hiss and a
splutter of summons to attention away
from the onions that are still making
me tear up and cry

at a nudge from the chief cook
I'm out and away to
the fridge at the back that has
never seen work like tonight
before the flurry of pastries to bake
with an aim for somewhere less than midnight
we might be doing ok but
they're burning and we're nowhere
near ready for the dishes to load
in the washer and the benches need
a wipe down to put preparations away
then to bed where there's more room
than the kitchen for two
and I'm tired so hold me a moment
then let's close our eyes
and goodnight till I see you
at first light again

2001

My Neighbourhood

pruning roses with an ally

last year the climbing rose had been neglected
it had spread to hide the roof line
entered inside the eaves of the house
required hard labour to cut back and extract
from the timbers of the eaves
this year will be more straightforward

there are noises in this house
through the night hours
brown brush tail possums -
the large variety -
not the more delicate grey ringtails
inhabit the vicinity and maraud
on a nightly basis
loud and clumsy bludgeon-creatures
of the after-hours

they leap to the roof with a startling thud
resounding like the clattered fall
of a dishevelled drunk
then a stumbling disport
in the ceiling and the walls
complete with grunts   defecation
and staining urine

they dislodge electrical mountings
and gnaw the wires   the warmth
of hot-water plumbing
an un-subtly sought attractant
during rest periods in the riot
of nocturnal disport

tender green shoots are a dietary supplement
left as abrupt   clean-bitten stumps
at the point where each shoot
becomes a little thicker
where the thorns perhaps present a challenge
to the sensitivity of a hungry pink mouth

pests and rest-depriving nuisances
these sleepy buffoons
but the prickly task of extracting
rose branches
from the depths of the eaves this year
will not be difficult

November 2001

My Neighbourhood

secret life of eucalyptus

the front-yard eucalypt is tall and mature
it is evergreen mustard-shaded taper-leaves
red blossom and gumnuts

the tree sheds bark and other old growth throughout the year
and when the wind blows from the north
as it is today
the ground carries as many as enough
of fallen twigs and dry branches

this tree embodies support
for a notion I have heard expressed
about a secret life of plants
about their capacity to experience pain
the possibility of them possessing feelings

in fact
I have now been startled into wondering
if there is not
an entire societal structure not yet explored
for a glance upwards towards the source
of so much casually discarded refuse
reveals a dry branch twisting in the wind
clinging with the tip of a tortured tendril
to an extrusion out-thrust
from a branch further above
it is a plaintive scene full of pathos
and desperation
beyond the grasp of my reach

I am left to watch and to wonder
did it fall
or jump

was it perhaps
pushed

2002

Frank Prem

shadow, light and springtime

the pink blossoms have a cold-ice quality
in the shadows where sunlight
does not penetrate
a damp darkness prevails
among the small forest
of pencil-thin branches striving upwards
where the sun strikes there is candy-warmth
and delicate shades of springtime

looking into the sun from beneath a canopy
of overhanging branches that hum of bees
the pink becomes white
barely countering the strength of light
that streams out of a cloudless morning

my shoulders are covered
in discarded blossoms
I too am entering springtime

August 2002

My Neighbourhood

singing broken heart at number 60

I frighten the neighbours
with sweet songs of love
the only way to sing them
is loud

I don't suppose
what they hear
sounds much like most love songs
but what would they know
of the way I resound
with heartfelt emotion
when I sing melody
to emmy-lou's lead

and elton and I
know each other from way back
dirt cowboys and strugglers
with nothing to lose

the boss is the man
to tell a true story
he sings slow and low
and I reach for the deep notes
to stop him from being alone

I guess the neighbours
have a right to feel puzzled
for I give no clues by appearance
that I can sing broken heart

looks are deceptive
and the lounge is a hotbed
of loving and hurting
sweethearts and cheaters
and I am the man
who sings a loud melody
when emmy-lou leads

May 2003

sniffer beagle

on my last return to this country
passing through customs
I made the acquaintance of a beagle
wearing a burgundy coat
and an inquisitive nose

he sniffed my trolley
then my bags and my feet

hard to tell from his face
but the wagging tail suggested pleasure
in welcoming me back home

he sniffed my crotch

I was happy to be back

tonight on the television
the same dog
the same coat
the same happily wagging tail
the same willingness to sniff
everything

I believe that beagle
is a touch promiscuous

I am hurt

November 2001

My Neighbourhood

the buds of rose

there are six

the lowest leans forward
to caress the climbing trellis

higher up the next strives to the right
waving in slight breeze

two hug the brickwork
on the wall of the house

the fifth is showing pink
through a slight split in enfolding green

the last is pointing to the sky
for there are no limits to the reach
of the inquisitive

September 2001

the churchill avenue push

take notice that
this avenue is closed
to low level flight

from first chortle
to the call at sundown
the road between
the corner and the bend
is off limits

the gang is in control
and the "push" doesn't take lightly
to rule breakers
or any casual passing by

fence scouts are posted
each end of the turf
watching out for trouble
that better not be you
they know ways
of making things unpleasant

bachelors every one
the big boys are smart strutters
walking to symbolise elite
so let the pheasants fly
if that's the best
they can do

> *who let that pigeon land?*
> *go take its name and number*
> *what a cheek*
> *we'll have no more*
> *of these peckings of rebellion*

My Neighbourhood

black and white
you better wear
the colours
if you want to walk
the avenue

black and white
if you're not magpie
you're nothing

2001

the flame tree has flowered

the flame tree has flowered
a striking contrast
between the vivid red of the stalk
and clusters of flowers
hanging in clumps like berries on a bush
and the pale green foliage

from a distance the tree
is covered in splotched gashes
red as blood
catching the eye with colour

up close it is ugly

February 2002

My Neighbourhood

the rumble of morning

it is like the sound of the earth
brushing through the stilled stark silhouettes
of post-daybreak morning
that surround the bedroom window
to embrace sleepers
gently   persistently
shake them and speak
in a familiar
slow
rumbled monotone
of waking and work
and the building urgency
that is the rising day

then gone

at the first response
of rising and showers
sound rattled in the kitchen
and a house awake
coming alive
it is gone

only six days in seven
sunday is a day of rest
even for a rumble
that seems to rise
like the sound of the earth

June 2002

under my southern sky

there's an aura
just above the roofline
of a neighbours house

it is chelsea down there
holding a glow
against midnight
but above my head
the pointers lead my eye
to the southern cross
and I feel good inside
to be in aspendale
under my southern sky

the crickets preep-preep
preeping is the only sound
I suppose the parties
have gone to bed
leaving me alone
with an aura
and some pointers
and a cross
that marks the stars
that make this my home
beneath the southern sky

February 2003

willow lights

the ornamental willow is still bare of leaves
its branches form a mat of curling chaos
where tree overhangs house
sillhoueted starkness that moves gentle
like a murmur in the remnant breeze
of a day of storm violence and bluster

away from the line of vision a street-lamp
scarcely disturbs the sombre colour of night
but catches a point in each twist of branch
to reflect a glitter of wavering fairylights
that lighten the sodden air of late winter
and suggest a wonderland in the front yard

August 2001

willow nine tails

for months the ornamental willow
has been a lifeless mass of twisted branches

today green protrusions
transform dead sticks
into hinted writhing energy

a sinuous cat of nine tails
to flay the back of winter

September 2001

After Words

Index of Poems

A

acting on one leg 163
a disparity of views 195
advice 74
a feeling for song 5
a fragment of clouds 196
after his women 164
a hum for you 6
all anyone can ask 166
a man called merry christmas 161
an accustomed gaze 168
an aspendale chorus 206
an avian reminder of cold 207
and so to work 99
an empty theatre 98
a new cloud 197
another familiar layer 208
april fools day flyers 209
april moon 75
a private eye 198
a resemblance 199
a rural autumn 97
a song in the dark 7
a sound of home 200
a spring smoke ring 201
assertive gestures 169
a summer 202
a surprise of iris 204
at doyle's 170
at the armadillo 100
a wailing companion 8
awaiting a call to arms 210
axeman blues 172

B

baby's bedtime 173
bamboo and reed 10
bamboo breeze 11

black cloud low 205
blossom possum 212
blur day 213
born to dance 214
brassy slow time (will you dance?) 12
brisbane trees 101
broke-neck guitar 13
burned in love (yee haw!) 14
busy day clouds 215

C

call for an inquiry 216
call it music 16
capturing magic 77
chick magnet 217
choir and accompaniment 103
choosing between guitars 17
circle dance 18
cockle bay 19/08/02 106
company for a magpie 219
composition 79
coriander 220
creation study 29
crushed flowers 222
curtain down (for jenny langley) 174
curves add character 30

D

dancer 177
dangerous decor 20
days of affirmation 80
dead shrub 223
don't ring before seven 175
dot point poetry 81
dress sense 31

E

easter parade weather 108
especially with music 21
essentially enigma 33

F

fashion cleanser 34
friday marching 110

G

ghosts 224
gippsland traveller 112
going coo-coo 225
grinning in shadow 226
gunshot 227

H

harbinger 228
hypothesis 229

I

ink, pastel and water 35
in song and silence 22
in the rehearsal room 23
iris and orchid 37

J

jen 179
joe pretty-words 82
just a lifeline 84

K

kinds of nothing 85

L

late shift and the lonely bull 26
less than average rain 230
little stories 86
lollypop man 180
long distance writer 87
lygon street 114

M

magpie submission 231
male nude 38
man of flowers 90
marked - nothing to say 91
mcg (black and white and blues) 117
meteorology - a love story of melbourne 115
mietta o'donnell 181
minor adaptation 232
modest art 39
moorabbin airport, july 29, 2002 120
mysterious woman (and duck) 233

N

non-photographic south 121
no shortage 92
not better than this 122
nothing much wrong with that 93

O

old trevallion 182
oncer 94
on charman road 124

P

painted daybreak 40
paradise falls 125
pebbling brown 126
perhaps a long spring 127
permootations of light and shade 41
perpetually young 183
picture on a wall 42
picture window 235
pink snow 234
pink throb latte 129
pink upon the avenue 131
pleasure complex 132
poet in the rubble (of 9/11) 53
poetry on saturdays 54
portraiture 43

praying for grandfather 184
pre-meeting at the grace darling, collingwood 135
preparations (two in the kitchen) 236
pruning roses with an ally 237

Q

quasi-cosmopolitan coffee 137

R

reading modern poets 56
resigning from australia 138
rhymer 58
ronnie's other guy 186

S

school soiree - act 1 142
school soiree - act 2 143
school soiree - act 3 144
sculpting in spanish 44
secret life of eucalyptus 239
shadow, light and springtime 240
signal for a sighting 145
sing calligraphy 45
singing broken heart at number 60 241
sky points 46
sniffer beagle 242
study of a canberra fountain 146
summer parchment 47
supportive analysis 59

T

teller of small tales 62
telling the come-what-may 63
tell them anything 60
tell you a story 61
the age of poetry 65
the churchill avenue push 244
the flame tree has flowered 246
the letter nothing 66
the limitations of weather forecasting 147

the ms society sparrow 148
the osteo 187
the pretty valley 150
thereafter 69
there's codfish at yarrawonga 152
the rumble of morning 247
the storyteller 67

U

under my southern sky 248
under the red dust 154

V

value for money 189
visitors 156

W

whose six-pack? whose scotch? 190
willow lights 249
willow nine tails 250
words and music 70
working on a phrase 72
writing and saying almost anything 73

Y

yellow roses 49

Author Information

Frank Prem has been a storytelling poet since his teenage years. He has been a psychiatric nurse through all of his professional career, which now exceeds forty years.

He has been published in magazines, online zines, and anthologies in Australia, and in a number of other countries, and has both performed and recorded his work as spoken word.

He lives with his wife in the beautiful township of Beechworth in North East Victoria, Australia.

Connect with Frank

Find Frank at his website www.FrankPrem.com, or through Social Media online at Facebook, X (Twitter), Instagram and YouTube.

Other Published Works

A Poetry Archive

A Poetry Archive – Volume 1 (2024)
A Poetry Archive – Volume 2 (2024)
A Poetry Archive – Volume 3 (2024)
A Poetry Archive – Volume 4 (2024)
A Poetry Archive – Volume 5 (2025)
A Poetry Archive – Volume 6 (2025)
A Poetry Archive – Volume 7 (2025)

Memoir

Small Town Kid (2018)
The New Asylum (2019)

Picture Poetry Series

Pilgrim Volume 1 - Illustrated by Leanne Murphy (2024)
A Lake Sambell Walk (2021)
A Few Places Near Home (2023)
The Unsuspected Slums (2026)

Children's Picture Books

The Beechworth Bakery Bears (2021)
Waiting for Frank-Bear (2021)
On Allium Avenue (2025)

Bachelard Interpreted

A Choir of Whispers (2024).
A Cleansing Flame (2024)
Real Weight (2025)
A Flight Of Ideas (2025)
An Ocean of Purity (2025)
The Kiss Reverberant (2025)

Speculative Poetry

The Garden Black (2022)
A Specialist At The Recycled Heart (2022)
The Cielonaut (2024)

A Love Poetry Trilogy

Walk Away Silver Heart (2020)
A Kiss for the Worthy (2020)
Rescue and Redemption (2020)
Alive Is What You Feel (2023)

Natural Disasters

Devil In The Wind (2019)
Of Drought and Fire (2025)
SMALL Change (2025)

War and Conflict

Sheep On The Somme (2021)
From Volyn To Kherson (2023)

Free Verse

Pebbles to Poems (2020)
White Whale (2024)
Ida: Searching for The Jazz Baby (2023)
Herja, Devastation With Cage Dunn (2019)

What Readers Say

Small Town Kid

A modern-day minstrel. Highly recommended.
—A. F. (Australia)

Small Town Kid is a wonderful collection.
—S. T. (Australia)

Devil In The Wind

Trust me, this book will stay with you. Bravo!
—K. K. (USA)

Moving, beautiful, and terrible. I was left with a profound sense of respect, as well as a reminder that we should never take for granted every precious every moment of life.
—J. S. (South Africa)

The New Asylum

Words can't do justice to the emotional journey I travelled in (reading this collection).
—C. D. (Australia)

If I had to pick one book over the past year that has truly resonated with me, this would be it.
—K. B. (USA)

Walk Away Silver Heart

Instantly grips you by the throat in his step-by-step story of survival. Bravo!
—K. K. (USA)

Outstanding!
—B. T. (Australia)

A Kiss For The Worthy

A Celebration of Life Written in Thoughtful Bursts of Poetic Expression
—C. M. C. (United States)

With every verse, I found myself reflecting about myself, my life, and the world.
—K.

Rescue and Redemption

The passion of love in its many forms explored by one for another.
—J. L. (United States)

I've enjoyed every word, every breath. Every moment within the life of these stories.
—C. D. (Australia)

Sheep On The Somme

Museums and archivists take note--sell this in your gift shops, preserve it in your archives. Professors, teachers--share with your students.
—A. R. C. (United States)

(This) book is a beautiful and graphic tribute to all those brave men and women who gave their lives for their countries between 1914 and 1918.
—R. C. (South Africa)

Ida: Searching for The Jazz Baby

I found myself deeply moved by the presentation of Ida's elusive, illusionary life.
—E. G. (United States)

He gives her a depth and vulnerability that the press didn't.
— A. C. (United Kingdom

The Garden Black

Prem creates verse that illuminates our world, its experiences and history.
—S. C. (United Kingdom)

Prem's poetry reminds that life is fragile and fleeting ... both harsh and beautiful.
—D. G. K. (Canada)

A Few Places Near Home

The author has captured many beautiful images in this book, and is a wonderful photographer as well as a poet. This book would make a beautiful coffee table book filled with moving prose to make us ponder with gorgeous accompanying images.
—D. K. (Canada)

www.FrankPrem.com

www.ingramcontent.com/pod-product-compliance
Lightning Source LLC
Chambersburg PA
CBHW052107110526
44591CB00013B/2392